FICTION, FOOD, AND FUN

Fiction, Food, and Fun

The Original Recipe for the READ 'n' FEED Program

Kathryn Closter, Karen L. Sipes, and Vickie Thomas

Foreword by Caroline B. Cooney

1998
LIBRARIES UNLIMITED, INC.
Englewood, Colorado

To the students of South Side Middle School,
but mostly to Jack Humphrey for his vision and inspiration,
and to Tyson, who has always loved dedications.

Libraries Unlimited, Inc.
P.O. Box 6633
Englewood, CO 80155-6633
1-800-237-6124
www.lu.com

Production Editor: Kay Mariea
Copy Editor: Jan Krygier
Proofreader: Suzanne Hawkins Burke
Design and Layout: Pamela J. Getchell

Library of Congress Cataloging-in-Publication Data

Closter, Kathryn, 1950-
    Fiction, food, and fun : the original recipe for the Read 'n' Feed
Program / Kathryn Closter, Karen L. Sipes, and Vickie Thomas ;
foreword by Caroline B. Cooney.
    xx, 224 p. 22x28 cm.
    Includes bibliographical references.
    ISBN 1-56308-519-4
    1. Reading (Middle school)--United States.   2. Middle school
students--United States--Books and reading.   3. Reading promotion--
United States.   4. Reading comprehension.   5. Middle school
libraries--Activity programs--United States.   I. Sipes, Karen L.,
1953-   . II. Thomas, Vickie, 1950-   . III. Title.
LB1632.C558   1998
428.4'071'2--dc21   98-9511
                                                              CIP

Contents

Foreword

Author visits are such a great way to see America—through its junior highs and middle schools. You never know, arriving at a school, what you'll run into. The marching band might be waiting on the sidewalk to greet you—or you might walk into the office and the principal will say, "And you're who? And you want to do what?"

Every now and then you have the privilege of finding deep, year-round enthusiasm for reading that pervades the entire school, sweeping up bright kids, bored kids, and at-risk kids; crummy readers and terrific readers; faculty of all disciplines; and parents who never thought they would volunteer in a reading program.

This was Anderson, Indiana, under the supervision of Kathryn Closter, Karen Sipes, and Vickie Thomas, and the book of mine that they chose to feature was *Flight #116 Is Down*.

Nowhere else have I been featured on a Flush Flash poster!

Nowhere else have I seen Celebrity Read posters in the foyer and halls—with the celebrity being a seventh grader, dressed in his older brother's football uniform, grinning joyfully over the book he just read.

I wasn't there for the Oreo Cookie challenge, but as an old Oreo Cookie fan, I'm sorry I missed it.

They'd had a Tag Team Read; the art teacher had read aloud during art projects instead of playing rock music; they used my books in a scavenger hunt to teach library use; and a hallway-long sheet of paper was used for a Response Wall for any editorial remark a reader wanted to make about the book.

But the highlight of the day was a READ 'n' FEED game played during lunch. Because *Flight #116* is a rescue story, Vickie, Kathy, and Karen designed Triage Bingo, and the winners got body parts. (Is this a good junior high activity or what?) I knew the answers, so I got a rubber Halloween eyeball, bloodshot and gross. Cool. I still have my eyeball.

Who had more fun at that READ 'n' FEED for *Flight #116*? Me, Vickie, Kathy, Karen, the Red Cross volunteers who demonstrated lifesaving, the teachers who pitched in with games, the parents, or the kids?

I got many letters from the students in the weeks and months following the visit. Every letter assured me that after reading the READ 'n' FEED title, the child had gone on to other books, other authors, other subjects—and couldn't wait for the next event. What more do any of us want than for our kids to rush into the library, glad to be there, eager to scoop up another book?

In my author visit journal (someday I'm going to break my silence and tell on the schools I visit: the funniest, the coolest, the most awful, the most wonderful) I wrote, "Anderson's READ 'n' FEED is impressive. Never have I met a librarian who has pulled off so much within her school system." And later in the year, having visited many more schools, I wrote, "Anderson was a hard act to follow, and sure enough, nobody else measured up."

In this book the authors have laid the groundwork for people who want to try the same activities. It's work, but the result is worth it.

The result is a lot more kids reading a lot more books.

Caroline B. Cooney
Westbrook, CT

Acknowledgments

The READ 'n' FEED program is the result of the creative efforts of many dedicated and talented people. We thank the following contributors for their work in developing this program:

The Middle Grades Reading Network, funded by the Lilly Endowment, Inc., for their leadership, networking, and funding.

The G.E.A.R. (Get Excited About Reading) Committee, in Anderson, Indiana, a citywide collaboration between East Side, North Side, and South Side Middle Schools and the Anderson Public Library.

The South Side Middle School Reading Motivation Team, particularly Amy Dishman, and the faculty and staff of South Side who became part of our community of readers.

Darla Staley and Myrna Fields at Owen Valley Middle School, who realized the potential of the READ 'n' FEED to motivate adolescents to read.

And our families for their generous help and unwavering support toward the development of this book, especially our computer guru, Ralph.

READ-N-FEED is a registered trademark of Micro Chemical, Inc. The term is used in this book in connection with a reading motivation program for adolescents with Micro Chemical's permission.

The Recipe for a Successful READ 'n' FEED Program

Author Jerry Spinelli writes in the foreword of *Books for You: An Annotated Booklist for Senior High Students* that he equipped Maniac Magee with "a bat in one hand and a book in the other," thus connecting a favorite activity (in this case, baseball) with reading. As we researched and experimented with ways to build a community of readers in our school and community, we also realized that such a connection could work for us. This book represents five years of linking books and pleasurable experiences with students.

The READ 'n' FEED program is a unique book discussion experience that features fiction, food, fun, and fellowship. The goals of this program are first to introduce a quality work of fiction to middle school or high school students and then to provide an opportunity for participation in a thoughtful discussion of it. Most important, students are encouraged to become lifelong learners by becoming involved in reading activities.

Each READ 'n' FEED features an appealing, popular young adult novel which the students read just before the event. Participants are divided into small groups of six to ten students who get acquainted over a meal, donated by a local restaurant or prepared by volunteers, and then engage in a discussion led by volunteer facilitators. The discussion format varies according to the selected title but may include games, role-playing, writing or art exercises, interviewing, or guest speakers. This program design allows for the exploration of innovative approaches to literature, unrestricted by classroom schedules, requirements, or environments. These programs have been successfully presented during lunch hours at our local middle schools and as dinner programs at the public library.

The success of the READ 'n' FEED program lies in its appeal not only to students who enjoy reading but also to students who are initially "lukewarm" about books but attend for the social opportunity. The outcome of the READ 'n' FEED experience is an awareness that reading and talking about books is fun! Students are given a dynamic opportunity to express their ideas and opinions outside a classroom setting. It is also an opportunity for the students to see reading skills advocated and supported by their community.

The program is popular with middle school students; it can be adapted to younger or older audiences. Students considered to be at-risk participate with success in this program through the assistance of supportive teachers who read the selected book to them. The resulting discussion is enhanced by the diverse points of view of students at widely varying academic levels and the added benefit of peer acceptance outside established circles.

Another benefit of the program structure is the opportunity it offers to parents and community members to be involved with students in a relaxed yet academically rigorous activity. Students enjoy expressing their opinions to adults who are there to listen but not evaluate, and the adult participants welcome the chance to demonstrate their interest and support of their students and the school.

Key Elements

The following paragraphs discuss some of the key elements necessary for a successful program.

DESIGN TEAM

We recommend creating a design team that will work to implement the READ 'n' FEED program. Our team consists of the school librarian, teachers from multiple disciplines, and a public librarian. Having team members from outside the school provides an avenue to create a communitywide program. Much of the success of this program can be traced back to a strong design team. Select individuals with unique talents or strengths that complement each other. A dynamic team will include at least one member who can initiate plans, one who is a creative thinker, one who enjoys attending to details, and another who can ensure that everything is completed on time. Students can add a valuable perspective to the design team, so do not hesitate to include them in your planning. The design team should meet regularly during the planning stages and at least once after the event to evaluate it. The length of time to plan a READ 'n' FEED will vary by title, but generally we are able to complete a broad outline of the theme and activities in one meeting. Each member of the design team then assumes responsibility for the details of at least one part of the program (e.g., publicity, decorations, or food) depending on his or her interests or skills. Our team finds it useful to document the planning experience and to record student reactions to the programming.

BOOK SELECTION

This process is great fun! The books we select for our programs are all by outstanding contemporary authors. We look for well-written books that have strong characters, genuine dialogue, and captivating plots or story lines. We glean our selections from book review sources such as *VOYA*, *School Library Journal*, and *Booklist*; recommended reading lists; book award lists; and student suggestions. Because we buy 50 to 75 copies of each featured book, we make sure our selected title is available in a paperback edition. We pay close attention to the gender of the main character so that we alternate between male- and female-dominated books. We also try to vary the reading level of the selected books; some selections are appealing to the lower reading levels in middle school, and others challenge the students to read beyond their grade level. The programs in this manual feature books from many genres. One of the benefits of this program is to introduce students to books they may otherwise miss.

FUNDING

There are many possible ways to fund a READ 'n' FEED. We use grant moneys, donations, and profits from schoolwide fund-raising campaigns. At the public library, the program is funded through grants and programming support from community organizations. This program is a perfect vehicle for involvement by civic organizations. Not only can these organizations help make the program possible, many may wish to participate in its implementation.

The largest expense is purchasing 50 to 75 paperback books of each title used. Because it is unlikely that a school or library will use a particular set more than once a year, it is practical and efficient to loan the sets out, thereby gaining borrowing privileges with another school. Our school has just two grades, 7 and 8, so we can repeat popular programs every other year. Most of the materials for the program are developed with a photocopier and student helpers to cut, sort, and staple.

FOOD

In the beginning, food was what drew students to this program. It still serves as an attraction, but now the activities we use to discuss the selected novel sustain the popularity of the program. We ask local businesses to donate lunch or dinner and are overwhelmed by their generosity. We also consider parent organizations and service clubs when looking for partners to provide food. The meal can be a creative part of the program, and you are sure to have fun figuring out ways to integrate themes, events, and people into what is served! If a particular food is mentioned in the novel, we usually try to have it as part of the meal. This leads to students trying new dishes, which adds to the fun. Other times, we rely on popular fast foods. We try to acquire the food donation as early in the planning process as possible so that we can include the donor's name on all publicity materials. Some meals will require cups, plates, and cutlery, which should also be gathered during the planning stages. We recommend serving the students cafeteria-style, using the discussion leaders and parents as servers and allowing the participants to eat while they discuss the book.

PUBLICITY

We find that one of the best ways to publicize a READ 'n' FEED is to let the students themselves spread the word. Their enthusiasm is contagious! We encourage students to help make posters and banners for the hallways, bulletin boards, and display cases. We always kick off our publicity with a booktalk over the public address system. When possible, we present student-produced video commercials, which are shown on our school network. These book commercials are a great way to grab the interest of students. We also produce "Flush Flashes"—so named because they are posted in the rest rooms. Flush Flashes use a newsy, tabloid approach that really gets the students talking about the program. In the library, we use displays to feature the selected novel. We extend the promotion to other works by the same author or books with similar themes. Colorful bookmarks with the READ 'n' FEED information are another good publicity tool. A feature article in the local newspaper or an article in the school newsletter are also great ways to increase community awareness of the program.

The actual sign-up for the program is held in the library. Students check out a copy of the novel and receive a copy of the Student Time Line Memo reminding them of deadlines. (They return the books to the library on the day of the program.)

TIME LINE

Once your planning group decides on a theme and activities, it is probably best to allow four weeks to complete all the preparations. Keep in mind that students may or may not need four weeks to read the selected novel. If the book is a "quick read," it is best not to let too much time elapse from the day the books are distributed to the day of the program so that students do not lose interest and enthusiasm. We always use a handout to inform the students of the deadline to sign up, date by which the novel must be completed, date of testing, and date of the preliminary program, as well as the READ 'n' FEED date. Generally, we require that the novel be completed and a comprehension test passed three to four days before the event. The preliminary program usually takes place the day before the READ 'n' FEED program. We find the best way to manage the list of who has books, who has finished reading, and who has taken and passed the test is through a user-friendly database management program. Our programs take place during 40-minute lunch periods at school or hour-and-a-half dinner times at the public library. We suggest activity times within the agendas in each chapter but we realize the times will need to be adjusted to fit your schedule and needs.

TESTING

Testing is a feature of the program that ensures student accountability. We find that this element helps students stay on track to complete the book before the discussion takes place. We use a computerized quiz that measures the students' comprehension of the novel. The software we generally use is produced by Electronic Bookshelf, Inc. [5276 S. County Road 700 West, Frankfort, IN 46041-8113, (765) 324-2182]. Another computerized reading management system is The Accelerated Reader produced by Advantage Learning Systems, Inc. [P.O. Box 8036, Wisconsin Rapids, WI 54495-8036, (800) 338-4204]. If a computerized quiz is not available for the selected title, we write a 20-question, multiple-choice quiz ourselves. Participants must score at least 80 percent on the quiz to receive a final invitation to the event. An alternative to testing may be to ask students for a verbal or written commitment to complete the novel prior to the program.

CONNECTIONS

One rewarding part of planning a READ 'n' FEED is making connections between the selected novel and our culture and community. We often brainstorm these connections using graphic organizers. We use the connections we identify for publicity, preliminary programs, discussion activities, and follow-up activities. Some novels have themes that we link to a familiar picture book, others we may link to current media such as films or popular music. For example, our students enjoy the connection between *Maniac Magee* by Jerry Spinelli and the creation of rap songs that reflect the themes, humor, and wisdom of the novel. The selected novels may have themes or incidents that connect well with local institutions such as museums, universities, cultural centers, or service organizations. For example, a good connection exists between the novel *Flight #116 Is Down* by Caroline B. Cooney and the work of the local American Red Cross organization. The connection may also be made to resource people in the community, people who have experiences pertinent to the theme of the book. This type of connection can be powerful as was the connection our students made between local Vietnam veterans and the novel *Fallen Angels* by Walter Dean Myers. The goal of establishing such connections is to expand the novel beyond the book covers into the lives of the students.

MOOD

Establishing a mood for the discussion is paramount for a successful READ 'n' FEED. The mood is built on key elements of the novel, which are expanded in the setting for the discussion. These elements may become part of the decorations, musical background, costumes for the facilitators, seating arrangements, discussion activities, or the meal. When planning for the physical arrangement of the room, be sure to allow enough space for activities to take place without distraction from nearby groups. We find that the students appreciate and enjoy the efforts we make to include in the event details from the novel. In fact, establishing the mood for the discussion is what distinguishes the READ 'n' FEED from other book discussions.

FACILITATORS

Discussion leaders, or facilitators, are vitally important to the success of this program. Students tell us that they like having the chance to express their ideas about a book to adults who simply listen rather than critique their thinking. We try to keep the discussion groups small, limited to approximately six students and one facilitator. The facilitator leads the group through the activities and encourages all to participate. Our facilitators are teachers, school administrators, librarians, community members, and parents. At our school, an entire department faculty will volunteer to be facilitators for a particular novel. This is an outstanding way for staff to demonstrate to students their support of the value of reading. This same commitment is apparent in the participation of parents and community members. A theme suggested by a selected novel may lend itself to participation by a particular community business or organization. We supply the facilitators with a copy of the novel as quickly as possible, and at least a week before the event we provide an outline of the activities, special instructions, discussion questions, game rules, and other relevant information.

One of the keys to the survival and success of our young adults is the realization of the importance of reading. Research has shown that providing access to current young adult literature, allowing time within the school day for free reading, and modeling positive reading attitudes will help create lifelong readers. We encourage you to become part of a network of reading partners who are making a difference in the lives of adolescent readers. Study the research on reading, become risktakers, and create ways for students to make connections between books and fun as they get excited about reading!

Using This Book

Each chapter of this book provides everything you need to conduct a READ 'n' FEED program. When used in conjunction with the information given here and in the appendix at the end of this book, the plans will facilitate a successful program. Each chapter presents all the information you need to conduct a memorable program in the following, standardized format:

- **Bibliographic Information.** This information can be used for ordering as well as determining the length of the book. We provide bibliographic data about the paperback edition as that is the edition most likely to be used.

- **Interest Level.** This is a key factor in determining the popularity of the novel with the students. The reading level of titles are generally between 6.2 and 9.6 (Fry Readability Scale).

- **Themes.** Themes are identified to provide planners with preliminary information about the content of the novel. This information may be useful in planning multidisciplinary units across the curriculum.

- **Plot Summary.** The plot summary offers a quick overview of the novel. Gender and age of the main characters are identified, as well as the major design of the story.

- **Author Information.** Students are curious about the lives of the authors of the books they read. This information can be used to promote the program or interest in other works.

- **Booktalk.** Booktalks are a great way to promote books to students! There are many sources for booktalks in addition to the examples we provide.

- **What's Cookin' at the READ 'n' FEED?** This paragraph provides readers with an overview of the program. The goals of the discussion are identified by providing a brief description of the activities.

- **Preparations.** This section provides lists of materials to acquire and tasks to accomplish before the event takes place. Always devise a seating plan that allows for the best random mix of students at each table.

  Shopping List. The materials necessary to implement the program are described and listed. Use this checklist to assign responsibilities to the design team.

  Adding the Garnishes. Suggestions for literature and other media connections are provided in this section, as well as community resources that work well with the novel.

  Food for Thought. Foods that are mentioned in the novel are listed here. Using any of these foods in the program contributes to its cohesiveness.

  Whipping Up the Fun. This section gives detailed information about the construction of the discussion "devices," activities, and decorations.

- **Whetting Their Appetite.** These activities are used to generate excitement about the READ 'n' FEED. They usually take place a day or two before the event and serve to focus attention on either the theme or an incident from the novel. The organization of the discussion activities and the expectations for participants are explained during the preliminary program.

- **Mixing the Fiction, Food, and Fun.** This section provides detailed information about the format for the discussion of the novel. Clear instructions are provided about games, role-playing, writing or art exercises, and any other processes recommended for the novel.

- **Hints for a Gourmet READ 'n' FEED.** Our recommendations for a successful program are based on our observations of many programs. Hints, suggestions, and inspirations are shared to enrich and benefit the planning process.

- **Novel Connections.** Follow-up activities are an excellent way to extend the success of the READ 'n' FEED. These connections can build bridges to community and cultural processes or events.

- **More Book Bites.** Our ultimate goal is to create lifelong readers, so we include additional titles that can be recommended to students who ask for more. The titles on the lists feature similar themes, characters, or events.

- **Templates.** The templates included in each chapter will provide users of this book with a complete set of materials for each READ 'n' FEED. These may be photocopied quickly and easily.

The appendix to this book provides READ 'n' FEED forms for use in planning and implementing a READ 'n' FEED program. The Planning Outline and Program Checklist as well as the Sample Student Time Line Memo and the Program Evaluation will help you implement, revise, and evaluate your program. The titles in the bibliography may provide you with inspiration and information as they did for us as we developed this program.

Chapter 1

The Dark-Thirty: Southern Tales of the Supernatural

Bibliographic Information

Patricia C. McKissack. *The Dark-Thirty: Southern Tales of the Supernatural.* Illustrated by Brian Pinkney. New York: Alfred A. Knopf, 1992. 122 pages. $12.00. ISBN 0-697-81863-4.

Interest Level

Grades 6 through 10

Themes

Family, Individuality, Horror, Ghosts, Prejudice

Plot Summary

The "dark-thirty" is that short time between daylight and dark when ghosts become a believable phenomenon. Inspired by the story-telling traditions of the author's family, the 10 original stories of the supernatural in this collection are set in the southern United States in the nineteenth and twentieth centuries.

Author Information

Patricia C. McKissack is the author of several award-winning young adult novels. In 1993, *The Dark-Thirty: Southern Tales of the Supernatural* was selected as a Newbery Honor Book and won the Coretta Scott King Award. She remembers listening to her grandmother tell deliciously horrible tales that made her spine tingle. McKissack has written another collection of stories called *Piece of the Wind: And Other Stories to Tell*. After graduating from Tennessee State University with a degree in English, McKissack became a teacher. Several years after she married civil engineer Frederick McKissack, they became a dynamic writing team. They published their first book together in 1984. Two of the books on which they collaborated were awarded the Coretta Scott King Award. They are *A Long Hard Journey: The Story of the Pullman Porter* and *Sojourner Truth: Ain't I a Woman?* Patricia and Frederick McKissack live in St. Louis, Missouri, and like to work in their garden during their leisure time.

Booktalk

Evil will not go where it is not welcomed, but it is a wily trickster that can cleverly gain invitation from its victims. When Laura came into my shop, I warned her not to take that sculpture home with her. Laura mumbled something about a "hideous toothless hag with burning silver-hot eyes" that she saw in the window of my shop, the Mother Africa Shop. She dismissed it as stress. But when she handed me the sculpture, I knew it was evil disguised, just waiting to be taken into the home of an unsuspecting victim like Laura! But she wouldn't listen to me. That's why I gave her the gingi. It was her only hope. The gingi was better than a rabbit's foot, better than a four-leafed clover, better than throwing a ton of salt over your shoulder. It could keep the evil from doing any harm . . . as long as she could unlock the key to its power.

What's Cookin' at the READ 'n' FEED?

Scenery depicting southern swamps and the front porch of a farmhouse create the appropriate atmosphere in which to experience *The Dark-Thirty* activities. The first activity, "Putting Feelings into Words," invites students to expand their emotional vocabulary. Next, students kick back and listen to a guest storyteller. Story swapping begins as students pair up and share a story about the strangest, scariest, or weirdest thing that has ever happened to them. For the final activity, students toss a ball of yarn around their circle as they collaboratively spin a yarn of their own.

Preparations

Read "The Recipe for a Successful READ 'n' FEED Program" at the beginning of this book for a discussion of those materials, designs, resources, and handouts needed for every READ 'n' FEED. Be sure to copy the Planning Outline and Program Checklist form in the appendix of this book, so you will have it ready for your first design team meeting. Specific to *The Dark-Thirty*, invite a storyteller and prepare balls of yarn, sets of characters lists, and cards for each table.

SHOPPING LIST

- Construction paper: black, brown
- Table coverings, plates, napkins, cups, dinnerware as needed
- Baskets, balls of yarn
- Materials for decorations: pin oak leaves, Spanish moss, battery-operated lanterns, picket fences, white sheets

ADDING THE GARNISHES

- National Storytelling Association, P.O. Box 309, Jonesborough, TN 37659, (800) 525-4514.
- Van Allsburg, Chris. *The Mysteries of Harris Burdick.* Boston: Houghton Mifflin, 1984.
- ————. *The Portfolio Edition of The Mysteries of Harris Burdick.* Boston: Houghton Mifflin, 1996.

FOOD FOR THOUGHT

A menu for this event can include any and all of the foods mentioned in the 10 stories: grapes, fresh-squeezed orange juice, fresh biscuits, ham, eggs, grits, lemonade, tomatoes, carrot sticks, apples, and apple pie. Sometimes pizza as a main entree works well with samplings of foods from the book that the students might not otherwise try.

WHIPPING UP THE FUN

Publicize the program. Copy the publicity poster (Template 1.1) and the Flush Flash (Template 1.2). Add local event details before displaying these promotional templates. Write a student announcement using the sample from the "Booktalk" section of this chapter. Distribute books to the students with a schedule of event dates and expectation deadlines. (See the sample Student Time Line Memo in the appendix at the end of this book.)

Select facilitators and give each of them a copy of the novel to read. At least a week before the program, supply the facilitators with any special instructions, the Characters List (Template 1.14), a copy of the Emotion Cards (Templates 1.15a and 1.15b), and Agenda and Activity Instructions (Template 1.16).

Invite a storyteller to prepare a short performance to model his or her art before the entire group.

Procure as many copies as you will have tables of the picture book or portfolio edition of *The Mysteries of Harris Burdick* by Chris Van Allsburg. The portfolio format contains 12-x-16-inch sheets of the illustrations for each table to use as story starters for the "Spinning a Yarn" activity.

Copy *The Dark-Thirty* Characters List (Template 1.14), and prepare a set of Emotion Cards from Templates 1.15a and 1.15b for each table.

Plan and prepare decorations to create an eerie mood. The setting could be the front porch of a southern farmhouse at "dark-thirty" with white picket fences like those used around a garden, Spanish moss, and a rocking chair; or re-create the look of a story-telling festival with wood stumps around mock campfires. Design a different look for each table based on the stories in the collection. Choose as many different table signs from Templates 1.4 to 1.13 as your attendance requires. Put decorations on each table that relate to the story. For example, for the table signed "The Legend of Pin Oak," find pin oak leaves to scatter in the center of the table as decoration. In "The Conjure Brother," Madam Zinnia's table is complemented with fresh-cut flowers, a sunny-looking tablecloth, and items that might be expected in a conjure woman's house, such as small bottles with colored water labeled as potions. "The 11:59" table can be decorated like a dining car on a passenger train: white tablecloth, napkins, and utensils set according to etiquette.

Copy and cut apart the invitation, Template 1.3, which students receive as their admission. Deliver these invitations the morning of the activities.

Copy and cut apart the Table Tickets, Template 1.17, to be used at the door. Students exchange their invitations for table tickets that designate their seat assignments.

Copy the Agenda and Activity Instructions, Template 1.16, and assemble the facilitators' packets. Each packet should include a place card with the facilitator's name, a copy of *The Dark-Thirty* and *The Mysteries of Harris Burdick*, and a thank-you note. Place a packet at each table.

Whetting Their Appetite

The Dark-Thirty is a rich selection because the 10 stories are more than just scary. The author punctuates the stories with historical and political moments that might stimulate in-depth discussions concerning various issues. To begin, select one of the following program ideas to prepare your students for *The Dark-Thirty*.

- Invite a storyteller to do a short workshop with the participants.
- Booktalk other story collections of the same genre.
- Sponsor a ghost story contest, with the name of the winner to be announced at the READ 'n' FEED.
- Research topics discussed in the stories. Locate art, photographs, music, or other books that illuminate the topics. For example, find pictures of the Pullman cars and research the history of the Pullman porters, the Montgomery Bus Boycott, the Underground Railroad, the Kennedy and King assassinations, or the legend of the Sasquatch. Design a display incorporating the materials and information found.

Mixing the Fiction, Food, and Fun

Students enter with their passes, exchange them for tickets that designate their table assignments, pick up their food, and find their seats. Facilitators are in place, introductions are made, and the first activity, "Putting Feelings into Words," begins. Begin by reviewing the Characters List. Then have each student choose a different character from the list and an Emotion Card from the basket to complete this sentence: "(Character) felt (emotion) when (plot event)." The students should expand their emotional vocabularies by using one of the less familiar synonyms.

This activity is followed by the guest storyteller, who will tell a tale or two in 10 minutes tops! The storyteller provides a smooth transition into the third activity, "Story Swapping." Students at the tables pair and share a story about the strangest, scariest, weirdest, funniest, or most embarrassing thing that has happened to them or to someone they know. This pair and share activity allows everyone to tell a story within a short amount of time.

Activity 4 gets everyone on their feet as each group forms a circle for "Spinning a Yarn." Use the picture book provided at the table, *The Mysteries of Harris Burdick,* as a catalyst. Facilitators begin a story by showing one of the pictures and reading the caption aloud. Holding the end of the yarn, the facilitator tosses the ball to a student. After the student catches the ball, he or she adds more to the story, then holds the end of the yarn, and tosses the ball to another student in the circle, who adds more to the story, and so on. Students keep spinning their yarn until the READ 'n' FEED master of ceremonies gives the one-minute warning. The last person holding the ball must provide the conclusion to the yarn before the minute is up.

Hints for a Gourmet READ 'n' FEED

- Set up a simple database to make it easier for you to verify student participation and attendance, student homerooms, book circulation, and student testing results.

- Carry out the theme in menu, decorations, and publicity. For example, drape furniture that won't be used with white sheets and hang blackout curtains on the windows to simulate dusk. Bring several indoor plants into the room. Hang Spanish moss and cobwebs.

- Ask facilitators to dress as characters from the stories.

- Make sure the guest storyteller receives a copy of the book and understands the limited time frame for the performance.

- Review the agenda and activities with the facilitators beforehand. Answer any questions they have.

- Don't forget to evaluate your program. Student and facilitator comments will help you revise and adjust future READ 'n' FEED programs. A sample evaluation form is included in the appendix at the end of this book.

Novel Connections

Select one or more of these follow-up activities to extend the success of the READ 'n' FEED:

- Visit *The Mysteries of Harris Burdick* Web site at http://www.hmco.com/vanallsburg/ where students are invited to write and share their stories.

- Plan a field trip to a local story-telling festival.

- Invite students to collect stories from their parents or grandparents.

- Commit a favorite story to memory and share it with an audience.

- Invite an artist to teach the scratchboard art technique, the technique used by Brian Pinkney in *The Dark-Thirty.*

More Book Bites

Aiken, Joan. *A Fit of Shivers: Tales for Late at Night.* New York: Delacorte Press, 1992.

———. *A Foot in the Grave.* Illustrated by Jan Pienkowski. New York: Viking, 1991.

———. *Give Yourself a Fright: Thirteen Tales of the Supernatural.* New York: Delacorte Press, 1989.

Avi. *Something Upstairs: A Tale of Ghosts.* New York: Orchard Books, 1988.

Chambers, Aidan. *A Haunt of Ghosts.* New York: Harper & Row, 1987.

———. *Shades of Dark.* New York: Harper & Row, 1986.

Clark, Judith. *The Torment of Mr. Gully: Stories of the Supernatural.* New York: Henry Holt, 1990.

Cohen, Daniel. *The Restless Dead: Ghostly Tales from Around the World.* New York: Dodd, Mead, 1984.

Coville, Bruce. *Bruce Coville's Book of Ghosts: Tales to Haunt You.* New York: Scholastic, 1994.

———. *Bruce Coville's Book of Ghosts II: More Tales to Haunt You.* New York: Scholastic, 1997.

Gallo, Donald R., ed. *Short Circuits: Thirteen Shocking Stories by Outstanding Writers for Young Adults.* New York: Delacorte Press, 1992.

Gorog, Judith. *Three Dreams and a Nightmare: And Other Tales of the Dark.* New York: Philomel Books, 1988.

Hamilton, Virginia. *The People Could Fly: American Black Folktales.* New York: Alfred A. Knopf, 1985.

Hoke, Helen. *Horrifying and Hideous Hauntings: An Anthology.* New York: E. P. Dutton, 1986.

Jacques, Brian. *Seven Strange and Ghostly Tales.* New York: Philomel Books, 1991.

Jennings, Paul. *Unreal! Eight Surprising Stories.* New York: Viking, 1990.

Klein, Robin. *Tearaways: Stories to Make You Think Twice.* New York: Viking, 1990.

McDonald, Collin. *The Chilling Hour: Tales of the Real and Unreal.* New York: Cobblehill Books, 1992.

———. *Nightwaves: Scary Tales for After Dark.* New York: Cobblehill Books, 1990.

Richardson, Jean. *Beware! Beware! Chilling Tales.* New York: Viking Kestrel, 1989.

Schwartz, Alvin. *Scary Stories to Tell in the Dark.* New York: Lippincott, 1981.

———. *More Scary Stories to Tell in the Dark.* New York: Lippincott, 1984.

———. *Scary Stories 3: More Tales to Chill Your Bones.* New York: HarperCollins, 1991.

Yolen, Jane, and Martin H. Greenberg, eds. *Things That Go Bump in the Night: A Collection of Original Stories.* New York: Harper & Row, 1989.

Templates

Publicity Poster, Template 1.1

Flush Flash, Template 1.2

Invitation, Template 1.3

The Legend of Pin Oak Table Sign, Template 1.4

We Organized Sign, Template 1.5

Justice Sign, Template 1.6

The 11:59 Sign, Template 1.7

The Sight Sign, Template 1.8

The Woman in the Snow Sign, Template 1.9

The Conjure Brother Sign, Template 1.10

Boo Mama Sign, Template 1.11

The Gingi Sign, Template 1.12

The Chicken-Coop Monster Sign, Template 1.13

Character List, Template 1.14

Emotion Card (back), Template 1.15a

Emotion Card (face), Template 1.15b

Agenda and Activity Instructions, Template 1.16

Table Tickets, Template 1.17

READ 'n FEED

Dark-Thirty:

Southern Tales of the Supernatural

by Patricia C. McKissack

Where:

When:

Hungry for a good scare?

Check it out!

Template 1.1. Publicity Poster.

DARK-THIRTY

Date:_____

by Patricia C. McKissack

Supernatural Phenomena =

◆◆□ⅿ□■ⅽ◆◆□ⅽ●
□≋ⅿ■□□ⅿ■ⅽ

Can you figure out the following code from the clues above?

❋≋ⅿ ☺□ⅿ&■ⅿ◆◆
♠✳□■◆◆ⅿ□
♠ⅽ◆□◆ⅽ◆ⅿ≋
♦□□ ♠✳ⅽ□ⅽ
♌✶■♌✶
♚□♌♌♋□

Crack the Code!

Sponsored by

Story Ideas

What's the scariest thing that ever happened to you? What was your most embarrassing moment? Do you believe in ghosts? Have you ever seen a UFO? What's your favorite campfire story?

Don't forget to sign up for The Dark-Thirty READ 'n' FEED by:

Patricia McKissack's collection of 10 original stories are sure to make goosebumps. The illustrations by Brian Pinkney are done by an art technique called scratchboard. Check it out!

Southern Tales of the Supernatural

Template 1.2. Flush Flash.

From *Fiction, Food, and Fun.* © 1998. Closter, Sipes, Thomas. Libraries Unlimited. (800) 237-6124.

by Patricia C. McKissack

Congratulations! You've enjoyed the fiction; now it's time for the food and fun!

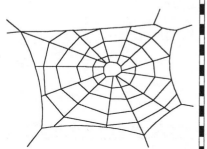

Where:

When:

READ 'n' FEED Pass:

by Patricia C. McKissack

Congratulations! You've enjoyed the fiction; now it's time for the food and fun!

Where:

When:

READ 'n' FEED Pass:

Template 1.3. Invitation.

From *Fiction, Food, and Fun.* © 1998. Closter, Sipes, Thomas. Libraries Unlimited. (800) 237-6124.

Template 1.4. The Legend of Pin Oak Table Sign.

Template 1.5. We Organized Sign.

Template 1.6. Justice Sign.

Template 1.7. The 11:59 Sign.

Template 1.8. The Sight Sign.

Template 1.9. The Woman in the Snow Sign.

Template 1.10. The Conjure Brother Sign.

Template 1.11. Boo Mama Sign.

Template 1.12. The Gingi Sign.

Dark-Thirty

Template 1.13. The Chicken-Coop Monster Sign.

Dark-Thirty Characters

"The Legend of Pin Oak"

Harper McAvoy * Henri Amos * Charlemae *
Mr. Kelsey * Benjamin Stone * Olive Hill * Mary DuPriest

"We Organized"

Ajax * Massa * Pappy Sims * Lilly Mae * Sally * Lee *
Corbella

"Justice"

Riley Holt * Miz Holt * Hoop Granger * Chief Burton Baker *
Alvin Tinsley * Miz Jasper's cat

"The 11:59"

Lester Simmons * Daddy Joe * Tip Samson

"The Sight"

Amanda * Esau * Tall Mayes * Charity Rose * the twins

"The Woman in the Snow"

Grady Bishop * Billy * Ray Hammond * Ray's wife * Eula
Mae Daniels

"The Conjure Brother"

Josie Hudson * Mama * Daddy * Arthur Lee * JoBeth * Miz
Annie * Miz Charlene * Madam Zennia * Adam

"Boo Mama"

Leddy * Germaine * Joe Morrison * Nealy *Sylvia * Sheriff
Martin * Jay Wilson * Dr. Jamison * Boo Mama

"The Gingi"

Laura Bates * Lizzie * Mrs. Aswadi * Jack * Thomas Lester *
Mr. Feathers * August * Dabobo

"The Chicken Coop Monster"

Melissa * Mama * Daddy * Ma Franky * James Leon Russell
(Daddy James) * Jay * Tissy * Mae Lizabeth * the Harper
children

Template 1.14. Character List.

Dark-Thirty:
Southern Tales of the Supernatural
by Patricia C. McKissack * Illustrated by Brian Pinkney

EMOTION CARD

Dark-Thirty:
Southern Tales of the Supernatural
by Patricia C. McKissack * Illustrated by Brian Pinkney

EMOTION CARD

Dark-Thirty:
Southern Tales of the Supernatural
by Patricia C. McKissack * Illustrated by Brian Pinkney

EMOTION CARD

Dark-Thirty:
Southern Tales of the Supernatural
by Patricia C. McKissack * Illustrated by Brian Pinkney

EMOTION CARD

Dark-Thirty:
Southern Tales of the Supernatural
by Patricia C. McKissack * Illustrated by Brian Pinkney

EMOTION CARD

Dark-Thirty:
Southern Tales of the Supernatural
by Patricia C. McKissack * Illustrated by Brian Pinkney

EMOTION CARD

Dark-Thirty:
Southern Tales of the Supernatural
by Patricia C. McKissack * Illustrated by Brian Pinkney

EMOTION CARD

Dark-Thirty:
Southern Tales of the Supernatural
by Patricia C. McKissack * Illustrated by Brian Pinkney

EMOTION CARD

Dark-Thirty:
Southern Tales of the Supernatural
by Patricia C. McKissack * Illustrated by Brian Pinkney

EMOTION CARD

Dark-Thirty:
Southern Tales of the Supernatural
by Patricia C. McKissack * Illustrated by Brian Pinkney

EMOTION CARD

Template 1.15a. Emotion Card (back).

ANGER

fury, ire, wrath, indignation, displeasure, enrage, incense, infuriate, outrage, exasperate, irritate, offend, rankle, vex

STRONG

forceful, zeal, zealous, hale, hardy, muscular, brawny, mighty, powerful, stalwart

SUSPENSE

anticipation, anxiety, expectation, tension, uncertainty

HAPPY

cheerful, content, delighted, glad, pleased, fortuitous, fortunate, lucky, opportune, seasonable, timely

FEAR

apprehension, misgiving, qualm, trepidation, dread, fright, horror, phobia, terror, awe, respect, shudder at, tremble at

JEALOUS

envious, covetous, resentful, possessive, protective, suspicious

HELPLESS

defenseless, dependent, disabled, feeble, impotent, incapable, powerless, abandoned, deserted, exposed, neglected

HATE

abhorrence, enmity, hatred, loathing, malice, malignity, vengeful, malevolent, malicious, rancorous, spiteful, venomous

SAD

dejected, depressed, melancholy, sorrowful, cheerless, dismal, lonely, lamentable, pathetic, pitiful, touching

LOVE

admiration, devotion, passion, regard, respect, affinity, attachment, esteem, altruism, eros, philos, agape, adoration

Template 1.15b. Emotion Card (face).

READ 'n' FEED

Dark-Thirty

Agenda

_____	(10 min.)	Serve and seat participants; begin eating
_____	(10 min.)	"Putting Feelings Into Words"
_____	(2 min.)	Introduction of Storyteller
_____	(10 min.)	Storyteller
_____	(10 min.)	Story Swapping
_____	(10 min.)	"Spinning a Yarn"
_____	(3 min.)	Wrap up and dismissal

Activity Instructions

Facilitators: This is a working lunch. Begin activities as soon as your group arrives at the table.

PUTTING FEELINGS INTO WORDS:
Review each of the stories with the "*Dark-Thirty* Characters" list and show the illustrations from the book to help students recall their reading. Have a student choose an Emotion Card from the basket, then complete the rest of statement: (Character) felt (emotion) when (plot event).

STORYTELLER:
Kick back and listen to the guest storyteller, who will tell a tale or two in 10 minutes tops!

STORY SWAPPING:
Students at the tables pair and share a story about the strangest, scariest, weirdest, funniest, most embarrassing thing that has happened to them or to someone they know. This pair and share activity allows everyone to tell a story within a short amount of time. If you have an uneven number of students at your table, pair and share with one of the students.

SPINNING A YARN
Activity 4 gets everyone on their feet as each group forms a circle. Use the picture book provided at the table, *The Mysteries of Harris Burdick*, as a catalyst. You begin the story by showing one of the pictures and reading the caption aloud. Then pick up the ball of yarn. Holding the end of the yarn, toss the ball to a student. After the student catches the ball, he or she adds more to the story, holds the end of the yarn, and tosses the ball to another student in the circle, who adds more to the story, and so on. Keep spinning your yarn until the READ 'n' FEED master of ceremonies gives the one-minute warning. The last person holding the ball needs to provide the conclusion to the yarn before the minute is up.

Template 1.16. Agenda and Activity Instructions.

From *Fiction, Food, and Fun.* © 1998. Closter, Sipes, Thomas. Libraries Unlimited. (800) 237-6124.

Template 1.17. Table Tickets.

Chapter 2

Don't Look Behind You

Bibliographic Information

Lois Duncan. *Don't Look Behind You.* New York: Dell, 1990. 179 pages. $4.50. ISBN 0-440-20729-0.

Interest Level

Grades 7 through 10

Themes

Identities, Family Relationships, Self-Knowledge

Plot Summary

Seventeen-year-old April finds her comfortable life changed forever when death threats to her father, a witness in a federal case, force her family to go into hiding under assumed names and flee a hired killer.

Author Information

Lois Duncan had her first manuscript rejected at age 10 and published her first story at age 13! It appeared in a teen publication called *Calling All Girls* and earned her $25, which, in those days, was a lot of money considering that her friends got $.35 an hour for baby-sitting. Instead of going over to a friend's house to play after school, Duncan would run home to check the mail for news from a magazine to which she had sent an article. Many years and more than 500 articles later Lois Duncan has editors coming to her with special assignments. Her work regularly appears in *Ladies' Home Journal*, *Redbook*, *Woman's Day*, and *Good Housekeeping*.

Young adults readers will best know Lois Duncan not as a writer of magazine articles but as an author of suspense novels. *Ransom*, published in 1966, was her first young adult mystery. It established her as a forerunner in the genre of suspense and psychic phenomena books. *They Never Came Home, A Gift of Magic, I Know What You Did Last Summer, Killing Mr. Griffin, Stranger with My Face, Third Eye,* and *Locked in Time* are just a few of her books. Many of her adolescent novels have been honored as "Best Books" selections by the American Library Association or as state book award winners.

Although Duncan started college at Duke University in 1952, she did not earn her college degree until she was invited to teach a class in magazine writing at the University of New Mexico. Not only was she a lecturer for the journalism department, she was also a student! She now lives in Albuquerque, New Mexico, and is married to an electrical engineer. Like many authors, bits and pieces of her own life find their way into her writing. April in *Don't Look Behind You* is based on the personality of her daughter Kaitlyn. Shortly after the novel was published, Kait was shot to death driving home from a friend's house. Lois writes about the murder and the similarities between it and events from *Don't Look Behind You* in *Who Killed My Daughter?*

Booktalk

April Corrigan ceased to exist on a Tuesday afternoon in May. Her rebirth began at the end of a long dirt driveway that wound through a maze of trees and bushes to a rickety carport. Those things that had been her trademarks as a junior at Springside Academy—a promising career as a state-ranked high school tennis player, her long blonde hair, a relationship with Steve with whom she had a date to the prom—could no longer be a part of her life. She was entering the Federal Witness Security Program. Someone had taken a shot at her father in the courtroom where he was testifying during a drug smuggling trial, and now the witness protection program was doing what it had done for many witnesses and their families: wiping out their identities and moving them to Nowheresville.

Could you give up everything you like or are familiar with to start a different life in a different town with a different name to protect your family? April can't imagine giving up her former existence forever. Instead of accepting the fact that she will have to look, act, and live the way someone else says she must, April makes a selfish decision that places her family in danger. Would you make the same mistake? Find out why you and April will have to walk away and never look back! Read *Don't Look Behind You* by Lois Duncan and participate in the READ 'n' FEED activities.

What's Cookin' at the READ 'n' FEED?

The title of the *Don't Look Behind You* program is "Identities: What Makes You You?" Each discussion group is led through a short examination of the Corrigan family identities before and after they enter the Federal Witness Security Program. This prepares the participants to formulate questions they will ask characters in the activity "April Fools." In this activity, a takeoff on the 1950s television game show "To Tell the Truth," three facilitators assume the identity of a main character. Two of the three are impostors and answer questions either truthfully as the character would or falsely; one facilitator always answers truthfully, accurately, and in character. The student groups are encouraged to ask questions that will help them determine who is telling the truth. The activity is played with a panel of Aprils, a panel of Lizs, a panel of Loreleis, and a panel of Brams. At the end of the questioning, the discussion group that identifies the most characters correctly wins. This activity is great fun and provides an opportunity for students to examine the identities of the book's characters and to experience the thrill of exposing an adult as an impostor.

Preparations

Don't look behind you and wish you had read "The Recipe for a Successful READ 'n' FEED Program" at the beginning of this book! Refer to that introduction for a discussion of those materials, designs, resources, and handouts needed for every READ 'n' FEED. Be sure to copy the Planning Outline and Program Checklist form in the appendix of this book, so you will have it ready for your first design team meeting. In addition, the *Don't Look Behind You* program requires collecting identity items for the opening discussion; selecting and preparing facilitators to assume character roles; and creating a performance area for the "April Fools" activity.

SHOPPING LIST

- Construction paper

- Table coverings, plates, napkins, cups, dinnerware as needed

- Materials for decorations to complete one of the themes suggested in the "Whipping Up the Fun" section of this chapter

- Identity discussion items for each table (try to collect at least six items): an issue of *Seventeen* magazine; a Columbia Record Company order form/envelope; a Virginia state road map or a copy of the state map from an atlas; a white Porsche or black Camaro miniature toy car; a copy of a "fake" Social Security card, driver's license, and school transcript; potted spring silk flowers; a picture of a cocker spaniel or a dog tag

- Pencils or pens

- Prizes for the "April Fools" activity, such as candy, bookmarks, free fast food coupons, or copies of a Lois Duncan novel

- A karaoke or other portable microphone and amplification system

ADDING THE GARNISHES

- CDs or tapes of Disney theme songs: "Some Day My Prince Will Come," "When You Wish Upon a Star," "It's a Small, Small World," or the Mickey Mouse Club theme song.

- Sabbag, Robert. "The Invisible Family." *The New York Times Magazine* (February 11, 1996): 32–39.

FOOD FOR THOUGHT

Orange juice, of course, needs to be the drink of choice. For the main course, you might consider southern fried chicken or other foods of southern origin as the Corrigans lived in Virginia and Florida. Another possibility is a menu served by a local fast food restaurant. Particular foods eaten by characters are prime rib, seafood casserole, cheesecake, cheese and crackers, and popcorn.

WHIPPING UP THE FUN

Publicize the event. Copy the publicity poster (Template 2.1) and the Flush Flash (Template 2.2). Add local event details before displaying these promotional templates.

Write a student announcement using the sample in this chapter's Booktalk. Distribute copies of the book to students with a schedule of event dates and expectation deadlines. (See the sample time line memo in the appendix at the end of this book.)

Select facilitators and prepare them to assume a character identity for the "April Fools" activity. Complete the character group schedule on the facilitator's letter (Template 2.4) and furnish each facilitator with a copy of the letter, the appropriate character outline (Templates 2.5–2.8), the Agenda and Activity Instructions (Template 2.15), and the novel. A week before the program, supply facilitators with any other information or templates that will help them prepare for the activities.

Decide where the program will take place and plan a room arrangement to accommodate the "April Fools" activity.

Copy Template 2.17 for each discussion table. Trim the four character identity samples apart before arranging them on the tables with the other Identity Discussion items.

Organize and plan decorations. Create a setting for the prom, Grandparents' Day at school, or a tennis team banquet. Regardless of the theme decorations, collect and arrange the following items in the middle of each discussion table: at least six Identity Discussion items listed in the "Shopping List" section of this chapter if possible, plus individual copies of the four character identity samples (Template 2.17).

Enlarge Template 2.9 and copy it on construction paper. Trim the rectangles, fold each one in half, and use them during the "April Fools" activity as character group place cards.

Petition one of your facilitators to ham it up as the "April Fools" activity leader. Provide him or her with a copy of the leader's guide (Template 2.10) and all four character scripts (Templates 2.11–2.14) to prepare for this assignment.

Select a prize for the winners of "April Fools." Candy bars or copies of other Lois Duncan novels are favorites with adolescents. Be prepared with a tiebreaker should two or more discussion groups guess the most "real" characters.

Create a scheme for seating students. Consider using character names: Steve Chandler, Mr. Corrigan, Mr. Loftin, Max Barber, Jim Peterson, Sherry Blaugrand, Rita Green, Kim Stanfield, Mike Vamp, or Larry Bushnell. Design signs to place on each table displaying a different name on each sign. Create seating tags using the same names to pass out to students as they enter.

Copy Template 2.16. At least two copies per table will be necessary if four character groups are scheduled to play "April Fools."

Secure a karaoke or any other portable public address system. The Activity Leader and student group leaders will use the microphone during the "April Fools" activity.

Send copies of the invitation (Template 2.3) to each student who successfully completes your requirements for participation.

Assemble the facilitators' packets. Within each packet include a place card with the facilitator's name, the novel, the agenda and activity instructions, and the character outlines for April, Bram, Liz and Lorelei.

Check that the following materials are at each discussion table: the Identity Discussion objects listed in the "Shopping List" section of this chapter, the four samples on Template 2.17, table identification sign for seating, pens or pencils, copies of the Questions for Character Groups activity sheets (Template 2.16), and the facilitator's packet.

Whetting Their Appetite

Select one of these program ideas to prepare your students for the *Don't Look Behind You* READ 'n' FEED:

- Contact the local FBI office to arrange for an agent to read the novel and then speak to your group. Ask the agent to explain the Federal Witness Security Program, including when and why it was developed. The agent might also brainstorm with the students examples of the everyday problems and situations April will encounter in trying to assume her new identity.

- Develop a creative writing exercise to prepare the students for the READ 'n' FEED activities. Students pretend they have been given a new identity in the Federal Witness Security Program and will describe their new life: name, hometown, kind of home, parent's occupation, friends, activities, and any other lifestyle issues.

- Read aloud and discuss the article "The Invisible Family," a *New York Times Magazine* cover story about a family living in the Federal Witness Protection Program. Edit the article to fit your time frame.

- Booktalk other Lois Duncan suspense novels.

Mixing the Fiction, Food, and Fun

Disney theme songs provide background music as participants enter. Students receive seating tags as they check in. After getting their food, they find a seat at the table that matches their tag.

Facilitators begin the program with the Identity Discussion described on the Activity Instructions (Template 2.15). Students select objects from the middle of the table in response to the first question, continuing around the table until all of the items are described. Group discussion continues until time is called.

Part 2 of the program features the "April Fools" activity. The leader directs facilitators to explain the format of "April Fools" to their groups and announces which characters will *play* "April Fools." Time is given for students to write a set of questions for each designated character for use in quizzing the facilitator/actors. The object is for the students to gain enough information to decide which actor is the "real" character and which actors are the impostors. Although facilitators will have copies of the character outlines, they should only refer to them to check facts. The complete directions for performing the "April Fools" activity are included on Templates 2.10 and 2.15.

The program is concluded by polling the discussion groups to see which one(s) were not April fools but were most often correct in guessing the "real" characters. Prizes are awarded.

Hints for a Gourmet READ 'n' FEED

Set up a simple database report to make it easier for you to manage student participation and attendance, student homerooms, book circulation, and student testing.

Make sure the program is well organized. Stick to your character group schedule and have student group leaders in line waiting to quiz the character actors. You don't want to waste time waiting for people to move here and there.

During the planning stages decide how much time will be designated for the "April Fools" activity. About 10 minutes are needed to complete the script and the questioning for each character group. The students and facilitator/actors really enjoy this activity, so it would be better to schedule fewer character groups than try to rush each group's questioning. Make sure you announce which character groups will be a part of your program before beginning "April Fools."

The better the facilitators who are assuming identities for "April Fools" know their "characters," the more at ease and convincing they will be at fooling the audience.

Don't forget to evaluate your program. Student and facilitator comments will help you revise future READ 'n' FEED programs. A sample evaluation form is included in the appendix at the end of this book.

Novel Connections

Select one or both of the following activities to extend the program.

- Read *Who Killed My Daughter?* Invite interested students to join in an informal discussion of similarities between this real tragedy and *Don't Look Behind You.*
- Show the video *The Client* (PG13), Warner Brothers, 1994. 121 minutes.

More Book Bites

Abercrombie, Barbara. *Run for Your Life.* New York: William Morrow, 1984.

Banks, Lynne Reid. *One More River.* New York: Avon Flare, 1996.

Beatty, Patricia. *Lupita Mañana.* New York: William Morrow, 1992.

Buss, Fran Leeper. *Journey of the Sparrows.* New York: Dell, 1993.

Duncan, Lois. *Who Killed My Daughter?* New York, Dell, 1994.

Nixon, Joan Lowery. *The Other Side of Dark.* New York: Dell, 1992.

Scoppetone, Sandra. *Playing Murder.* New York: Harper & Row, 1985.

Windsor, Patricia. *The Sandman's Eyes.* New York: Dell, 1987.

Templates

Publicity Poster, Template 2.1

Flush Flash, Template 2.2

Student Invitation, Template 2.3

Facilitator's Letter, Template 2.4

Character Outline for April Corrigan, Template 2.5

Character Outline for Bram Corrigan, Template 2.6

Character Outline for Liz Corrigan, Template 2.7

Character Outline for Lorelei Gilbert, Template 2.8

"April Fools" Signature Place Cards, Template 2.9

Guide for "April Fools" Activity Leader, Template 2.10

Character Script for April Corrigan, Template 2.11

Character Script for Bram Corrigan, Template 2.12

Character Script for Liz Corrigan, Template 2.13

Character Script for Lorelei Gilbert, Template 2.14

Agenda and Activity Instructions, Template 2.15

"April Fools" Questions for Character Groups, Template 2.16

Character Identity Samples, Template 2.17

What are your chances of seeing someone you know at Disney World?

READ 'n' FEED

Find out by reading this month's featured novel!

Sign-up:_____

(Date)

Room:_____

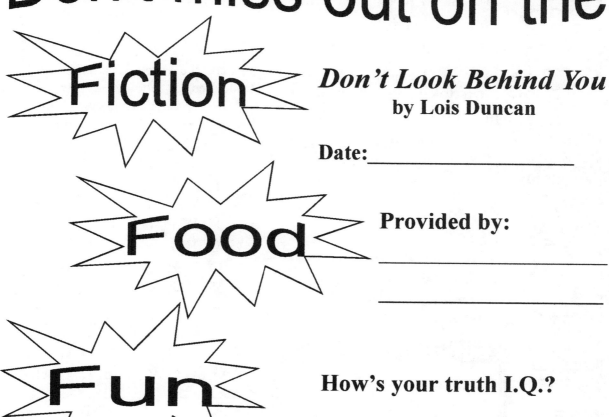

Don't miss out on the

Fiction

Don't Look Behind You
by Lois Duncan

Date:_____

Food

Provided by:

_____

_____

Fun

How's your truth I.Q.?

**Decide who the real April Corrigan
is in a game of "April Fools."**

Template 2.1. Publicity Poster.

From *Fiction, Food, and Fun.* © 1998. Closter, Sipes, Thomas. Libraries Unlimited. (800) 237-6124.

Don't Look Behind You

by Lois Duncan

Date:

Ever wonder what it would be like to leave everything that is familiar to you behind and disappear? People who go into the Witness Protection Program are asked to do just that. In *Don't Look Behind You,* April Corrigan can't forget about her past. She makes a mistake that endangers her family's lives.

Don't wonder what that mistake was! Plan to join the fiction, food, and fun in this month's READ 'n' FEED!

♦ **Be sure to read Lois Duncan's *Who Killed My Daughter?***

FLUSH FLASH

Fiction Becomes Reality

Kaitlyn Arquette, the author's daughter, was killed a month after *Don't Look Behind You* was published. Similarities between her death and the novel are remarkable.

In the novel, April was chased by a hit man in a Camaro. Witnesses told police that Kaitlyn's killers were driving a Camaro.

The hit man's name in the novel was Mike Vamp. The man indicted for shooting Kait was Mike Garcia, nicknamed Vamp.

Character Search

```
A B Z X I S L T U Q
R P M A S T O D C M
C H R P T E F E N A
G Q B I A V T V B K
L O R E L E I O S E
O N A R K L N U M N
F W M I K A T H K B
J I M D S R I T A G
W N A G I R R O C H
A G X C R Y E D N U
```

Steve	Loftin	Lorelei	Tom
April	Larry	Jim	Max
Bram	Kim	Rita	Corrigan

Template 2.2. Flush Flash.

CHARLOTTE COUNTY DEPARTMENT OF READING
GROVE CITY, FLORIDA

Certificate of READ 'n' FEED Registration

THIS IS TO CERTIFY **that, according to the records of this office**

Name _____
has successfully completed the requirements for *Don't Look Behind You*
and will be our guest on _____ Year_____
at _____ in _____,
_____.

Witnessed by:_____

Record was filed _____ Certificate No.__790__ Book__H-40__ Page__115

CHARLOTTE COUNTY DEPARTMENT OF READING
GROVE CITY, FLORIDA

Certificate of READ 'n' FEED Registration

THIS IS TO CERTIFY **that, according to the records of this office**

Name _____
has successfully completed the requirements for *Don't Look Behind You*
and will be our guest on _____ Year_____
at _____ in _____,
_____.

Witnessed by:_____

Record was filed _____ Certificate No.__790__ Book__H-40__ Page__115

Template 2.3. Student Invitation.

Don't Look Behind You

Dear Facilitator,

We look forward to your joining us on _____
for the READ 'n' FEED discussion and activities planned for *Don't Look Behind You* by
Lois Duncan.

The theme for the program is "Identities: What Makes You You?" In addition to
facilitating a short discussion of this theme at your assigned table, you will assume the
identity of April Corrigan, Liz Corrigan, Lorelei Gilbert, or Bram Corrigan as part of "April
Fools," a scenario similar to the television game show "To Tell the Truth." For this activity,
you will be seated with two other facilitators impersonating the same character. During
questioning from the panel of student participants, each of you will try to convince the
audience that *you* are the real April, Liz, Lorelei, or Bram. Check the schedule below for a
list of the other facilitators in your group and for your group's presentation time.

Decide among the three of you in your character group who will be the real character.
This person cannot step out of character or tell lies when asked questions from the audience.
The other two impostors may stretch the truth or purposely give misinformation. Included
with this letter should be a Character Outline for _____ to help you fool your
audience. Please add other facts to the outline to help you assume this character.

If you wish to dress up for your part in "April Fools," you might consider a tennis player
or high school girl in a prom dress, a rich, 50-ish woman who likes clothes and shoes, a
writer in sweats carrying some tools of the trade, or a little boy. The students will love
seeing you step out of your comfort zone to play these parts, so have fun with the role!

"APRIL FOOLS" CHARACTER GROUP SCHEDULE

GROUP A_____   April #1: _____
     (Time)   April #2: _____
          April #3: _____

GROUP B_____   Bram #1: _____
     (Time)   Bram #2: _____
          Bram #3: _____

GROUP C_____   Liz #1: _____
     (Time)   Liz #2: _____
          Liz #3: _____

GROUP D_____   Lorelei #1: _____
     (Time)   Lorelei #2: _____
          Lorelei #3: _____

Template 2.4. Facilitator's Letter.

Don't Look Behind You

CHARACTER OUTLINE FOR APRIL CORRIGAN

- Seventeen-year-old junior at Springside Academy
- Mother is a writer: Liz
- Dad works for Southern Skyways Airline: George
- Dad gives testimony in drug trial for F.B.I.
- One younger brother in third grade: Bram
- Dog: Porky
- Hometown: Norwood, Virginia
- Best friend: Sherry Blaugrand
- Boyfriend, whom she met at a Christmas party: Steve Chandler (drives a Honda Prelude)
- Grandmother: Lorelei Gilbert
- Aliases: April Gross and Valerie Weber
- Tall, long blonde hair that is cut short before moving to Florida
- State-ranked tennis player/doubles partner: Jodi
- Going to prom with Steve
- Receives crystal prism from Steve on 17th birthday
- Bedroom is known as "Princess April's Chamber": four-poster bed, oval mirror, rocking chair with blue cushion, camphorwood chest from the Orient
- Stays at Mayflower Hotel in Richmond for two and a half weeks, where hit man tries to get into the room
- Sends letter to Steve in Columbia Record Company envelope
- Enters Federal Witness Security Program and relocates with family to Grove City, Florida
- Meets Larry and Kim at tennis courts
- Kim's stepsister, Abby, recognizes April from plane trip
- Will not be able to play tennis for Grove City High School
- Sees Jodi at Disney World while on a mini-vay with family
- Returns to Norwood to see Steve and Lorelei
- Gets speeding ticket in Porsche on interstate
- Followed by black Camaro as she and Lorelei drive to Grove City
- Locked in closet at Grove City house on Lemon Lane and escapes through attic
- Knocks Mike Vamp in ditch with tennis racket

Template 2.5. Character Outline for April Corrigan.

Don't Look Behind You

CHARACTER OUTLINE FOR BRAM CORRIGAN

- ◆ Full name: George Bramwell Corrigan, Jr.
- ◆ Parents: Liz and George Corrigan
- ◆ Gets along well with his sister April
- ◆ Grandmother: Lorelei Gilbert
- ◆ Has one blue eye and one brown eye
- ◆ Dog: Porky
- ◆ Third grader at Crestwood Elementary School
- ◆ Favorite games are "Monopoly" and "Family Feud"
- ◆ Likes to add sugar to presweetened cereal
- ◆ Friend Chris was going to spend the night with Bram on Friday to watch "Nightmare on Elm Street" movies
- ◆ Believes that he and Chris are going to marry sisters and live together
- ◆ Leaves Norwood, Virginia, to go into hiding at Mayflower Hotel/watches television for entertainment
- ◆ Enters Federal Witness Security Program with family and moves to Grove City, Florida
- ◆ Wears contact lens or his Mickey Mouse sunglasses to disguise his eye color
- ◆ Visits Disney World with family on a mini-vay
- ◆ Alias: Jason Weber
- ◆ Goes to see the movie *Song of the South* with April the first day in Grove City
- ◆ Discovers trapdoors in the closets at the Grove City house on Lemon Lane and uses them to get into the attic to play

Don't Look Behind You

Template 2.6. Character Outline for Bram Corrigan.

Don't Look Behind You

CHARACTER OUTLINE FOR LIZ CORRIGAN

- Married to George/eloped against her parents' wishes
- Daughter: April, a tennis player
- Son: Bram, who has one blue eye and one brown eye
- Parents: Clyde and Lorelei Gilbert
- Came from well-to-do family
- Met husband at a ski resort in the Catskills
- Has short hair
- Writer of children's books
- Won the California Young Readers Medal and gave an acceptance speech at the state librarians' convention
- Graduate of Duke University
- Drives a Volvo station wagon in Norwood, Virginia
- Drives a Plymouth in Grove City, Florida
- Realizes husband has been working for F.B.I.
- Placed in Federal Witness Security Program after husband testified in drug trial
- Gets new birth certificate by the "dead infant" method
- Alias: Ellen Weber
- Eats a lot of seafood while in hiding at Mayflower Hotel/ room was on the 14th floor
- Doesn't really like her husband's friend Max
- Has coffee mug with I DO THE JOB WRITE printed on it
- Starts drinking in excess after relocating to Grove City, Florida: orange juice with vodka
- Goes on mini-vay with family to Disney World/leaves April and Bram while she and George go to 3-D movie at Epcot
- Determined to finish book she started before the family is moved to Florida
- George's new job in Grove City is running the fast photo processing shop called Zip-Pic on Maine Street
- Has fight with George about bringing home the typewriter from the shop
- Discovered that April wasn't at Kim's for the weekend
- Breaks arm when the car goes in the ditch the night Mike Vamp finds their house in Grove City

Don't Look Behind You

Don't Look Behind You

Don't Look Behind You

Template 2.7. Character Outline for Liz Corrigan.

From *Fiction, Food, and Fun.* © 1998. Closter, Sipes, Thomas. Libraries Unlimited. (800) 237-6124.

Don't Look Behind You

CHARACTER OUTLINE FOR LORELEI GILBERT

- Husband Clyde died from a heart attack while playing golf
- Daughter: Liz Corrigan
- Grandchildren: April and Bram Corrigan
- April always liked taking her to school on Grandparents' Day
- Slim, blonde hair
- Drives a white Porsche
- Lives in Golden Ridge Condominiums
- Security guard at gate is a man named Pat
- A socialite who likes expensive, fancy clothes
- Wears high-heeled shoes
- Graduate of Duke University
- Gave April antique furniture for her bedroom
- Picked April up from school the day her family went into hiding
- Sentimental items: porcelain doll, family Bible, photographs, honeymoon picture in France, ermine stole
- Does not wish to relocate with the Corrigans when they first enter the Federal Witness Security Program
- Takes care of Porky when the Corrigans leave Norwood
- Beat up by Mike Vamp/broken arm and bruised face
- Decides to go to Florida with April/misplaces map of their route to Grove City
- Locked in closet with April at the Grove City house on Lemon Lane

Don't Look Behind You

Template 2.8. Character Outline for Lorelei Gilbert.

Bram #3

Bram #3

Bram #2

Bram #2

Bram #1

Bram #1

Lorelei #3

Lorelei #3

Lorelei #2

Lorelei #2

Lorelei #1

Lorelei #1

Liz #3

Liz #3

Liz #2

Liz #2

Liz #1

Liz #1

April #3

April #3

April #2

April #2

April #1

April #1

Template 2.9. "April Fools" Signature Place Cards.

Don't Look Behind You

APRIL FOOLS
Guide for Activity Leader

Welcome the facilitators, guests, and participants. Ask facilitators to explain the format of the "April Fools" identity activity to their discussion groups. They should have the Activity Instructions in their facilitator's packet. Announce which characters will *play* "April Fools": April, Bram, Liz, and/or Lorelei. Give the groups five minutes to brainstorm questions they will want to ask these characters.

Begin the "April Fools" activity. Ask the first character group participants to take their places in the presentation area. Before being seated, each facilitator/actor states the "character's name" and you read a background letter from that character to the audience. The dialogue to use with the four different characters from the novel are included on the "April Fools" Character Scripts, Templates 2.11–2.14. (*Insert Part A of the appropriate script at this point in the activity.*)

Ask the actors to be seated and start the group questioning for that character. Monitor the questioning so that each discussion group has the opportunity to ask at least one question of the impostors. At the end of the allotted time, instruct the student groups to decide which person they think is the "real" character and state their reason for selecting that character impostor. (*Insert Part B of the script here.*) Invite the discussion groups to share their selections and reasons with the large group.

Following the group verdicts, ask the "real" character to stand. (*Insert Part C of the script here.*) The impostors should fake standing up to keep the audience in suspense! The "real" character finally does stand.

Thank the character group for its participation and call the next character group to come forward. Using the same format, lead "April Fools" for that character.

Keep the activity moving so there is little wasted time. Decide ahead of time the order in which the spokesperson from each discussion group will question. Do not allow any one discussion group to monopolize the questioning. Make arrangements for the second character impostor group to be "up front," ready to go, as soon as the first group is finished playing "April Fools."

Don't Look Behind You

Template 2.10. Guide for "April Fools" Activity Leader.

Don't Look Behind You

APRIL FOOLS
Character Script for April Corrigan

Part A

April #1:   *My name is April Corrigan.*
April #2:   *My name is April Corrigan.*
April #3:   *My name is April Corrigan.*
Activity Leader:

As a high school junior, I had everything I could want—close friends, a nice house, top seed ranking in the girls' state tennis tournament, a date to the Junior-Senior Prom with the boy of my dreams, and the perfect family. Today, none of that is true. I lost it all the day somebody fired a gun at my father in the courtroom where he had just testified in a drug smuggling case.

Signed,

April Corrigan

Part B

Activity Leader:

Audience, who is the "real" April Corrigan? Is it April #1, April #2, or April #3?

Part C

Activity Leader:

Now, will the real April Corrigan please stand up?

Don't Look Behind You

Template 2.11. Character Script for April Corrigan.

Don't Look Behind You

APRIL FOOLS
Character Script for Bram Corrigan

> Part A

Bram #1:   *My name is Bram Corrigan.*
Bram #2:   *My name is Bram Corrigan.*
Bram #3:   *My name is Bram Corrigan.*
Activity Leader:

My mom thinks I'm hyper. She's always telling me not to have too much sugar — no colas and go easy on the candy! I got pretty hyper the day I thought me, my mom, and my sister were going on a mini-vay. . .maybe getting to swim in a heated, indoor pool and eating whatever I want off a room service menu. Then I got pretty mad when I found out that I was leaving on a permanent mini-vay and wouldn't see my dog or my best friend Chris again. How can they do this to a kid?

> *Signed,*
> *Bram Corrigan*

> Part B

Activity Leader:
Audience, who is the "real" Bram Corrigan? Is it Bram #1, Bram #2, or Bram #3?

> Part C

Activity Leader:
Now, will the real Bram Corrigan please stand up?

Don't Look Behind You

Template 2.12. Character Script for Bram Corrigan.

Don't Look Behind You

APRIL FOOLS
Character Script for Liz Corrigan

Part A

Liz #1:   *My name is Liz Corrigan.*
Liz #2:   *My name is Liz Corrigan.*
Liz #3:   *My name is Liz Corrigan.*
Activity Leader:

From a storybook romance in which I eloped to marry the man I loved to my career as an author of children's fiction books, I have always found ways to escape from the challenges in my life that I didn't want to face. When my husband, George, came home one evening and told me that the F.B.I. had approached him about working undercover on a drug case involving his boss, he presented a threat to my peaceful, happy life. But not until Max appeared at our front door with news about George did I realize that the frightening fact was . . . I would no longer be writing fiction but living it!

Signed,
Liz Corrigan

Part B

Activity Leader:
Audience, who is the "real" Liz Corrigan? Is it Liz #1, Liz #2, or Liz #3?

Part C

Activity Leader:
Now, will the real Liz Corrigan please stand up?

Don't Look Behind You

Template 2.13. Character Script for Liz Corrigan.

Don't Look Behind You

APRIL FOOLS
Character Script for Lorelei Gilbert

Part A

Lorelei #1:   *My name is Lorelei Gilbert.*
Lorelei #2:   *My name is Lorelei Gilbert.*
Lorelei #3:   *My name is Lorelei Gilbert.*
Activity Leader:

I was an influential woman in my community of Norwood, Virginia. I was always the person called on to head the fund-raising projects. One day I did something very stupid. I opened the door to a stranger, and now my life has taken a painful turn.
Signed,
Lorelei Gilbert

Part B

Activity Leader:
Audience, who is the "real" Lorelei Gilbert? Is it Lorelei #1, Lorelei #2, or Lorelei #3?

Part C

Activity Leader:
Now, will the real Lorelei Gilbert please stand up?

Template 2.14. Character Script for Lorelei Gilbert.

READ 'n' FEED
Don't Look Behind You

Agenda

_____	(10 min.)	Serve and seat participants; begin eating
_____	(15 min.)	Identities Discussion
_____	(5 min.)	Activity instructions and question design
_____	(20-40 min.)	"April Fools" activity (approximately 10 minutes for each character group)

Activity Instructions

The theme for this program is "Identities: What Makes You You?"

As soon as all students in your group are seated, introduce the Identity Discussion. Ask students to respond to the following questions.

1. What were the symbols of the Corrigan family's former existence? Select an item from the identity objects in the middle of the table. Explain what the item is and to whom it relates.

2. What sacrifices did each character have to make to go into the Federal Witness Security Program? *April   Liz   Bram   Lorelei   George*

3. Suppose this is "The End of Your World Day." What do you think would be the hardest things to give up if you had to relocate and change your lifestyle like April did? *(Examples: home, friends, school, activities, hairstyle)*

Wait for a cue from the Activity Leader to explain to your discussion group the format for "April Fools." **Activity description:** "April Fools" is similar to the TV game show "To Tell the Truth." (You baby boomers will remember this show!) Three facilitators will assume the identity of one of the characters in the novel. They will each state their assumed name to the audience, and the Activity Leader will read a quote from that character. The character group will then be seated. Designated students from each discussion group will begin by asking questions of the actors to try to find out which person is the "real" character. The "real" character will always answer the questions accurately and truthfully as the character would. The other two impostors can stretch the truth or give an incorrect fact in response to a question. After the groups have the opportunity to question the characters, each group will select who it thinks is the "real" character and why.

The "April Fools" Activity Leader will guide you through this activity. He or she will direct your discussion group to generate a list of questions about specific people, places, and things related to the particular characters *playing* "April Fools". Choose someone in the group to be the recorder. Use your group's copy of Template 2.16 to write down the group's ideas.

Select someone else as the group leader to quiz the actors using one of the group's questions. Suggest that the same question be asked of two of the character impostors so that the audience can compare their answers.

Prizes will be awarded to the discussion group with the most correct "real" character guesses.

Template 2.15. Agenda and Activity Instructions.

Don't Look Behind You

April Fools

Questions to ask _____
                        (Name of character)

    1.

    2.

    3.

    4.

The "real" character is _____.   Why do you think so?   Were you correct?   Y   N

Questions to ask _____
                        (Name of character)

    1.

    2.

    3.

    4.

The "real" character is _____.   Why do you think so?   Were you correct?   Y   N

Questions to ask _____
                        (Name of character)

    1.

    2.

    3.

    4.

The "real" character is _____.   Why do you think so?   Were you correct?   Y   N

Template 2.16. "April Fools" Questions for Character Groups.

California Library Association

1988 YOUNG READERS MEDAL

awarded to

Liz Corrigan

. . . for her outstanding contributions to children's literature.

State librarians' convention
Young Readers Medal Luncheon
Sacramento, California
January 18, 1989

RICHMOND TIMES-DISPATCH

Volume 1   May 25, 1989 Richmond, Virginia

Local airline employee unharmed in courtroom shooting

George Corrigan, a 20-year employee of Southern Skyways, escaped injury in an attempt on his life yesterday as he left the courtroom following his testimony in a drug smuggling case. One shot was fired from the lobby stairwell by an unidentified man wearing a black leather jacket and stocking cap. The man fled from the building to a waiting car.

Corrigan was the government's chief witness to the smuggling operation run by Richard Loftin. On at least two occasions Corrigan accompanied Loftin to South. . .

NORWOOD GAZETTE

May 28, 1989   **Metro Section**   Morning edition

Deaths

NORWOOD — James R. Peterson, 59, Norwood, died May 27, 1989 in Richmond.

Born July 1, 1930 in Dale City, he lived in the Norwood area most of his life. He retired from the Norwood Police Department in 1984.

Survivors include his wife, three children, and seven grandchildren.

Services will be at 10 A.M. on Wednesday at the funeral home. Burial will be in Norwood Memorial Park Cemetery.

Memorial contributions can be made to the Federal Witness Security Program, Washington, D.C.

RICHMOND TENNIS OPEN

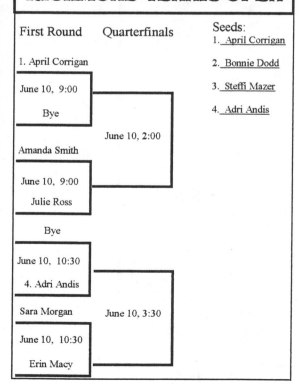

Template 2.17. Character Identity Samples.

From *Fiction, Food, and Fun.* © 1998. Closter, Sipes, Thomas. Libraries Unlimited. (800) 237-6124.

Chapter **3**

The Duplicate

Bibliographic Information

William Sleator. *The Duplicate*. New York: Bantam Books, 1990. 167 pages. $2.95. ISBN 0-553-28634-X.

Interest Level

Grades 7 through 10

Themes

Friendship, Individuality, Bioethics, Cloning

Plot Summary

Sixteen-year-old David, finding a strange machine that can create replicas of living organisms, duplicates himself and suffers the horrifying consequences when the duplicate turns against him.

Author Information

William Sleator is the author of young adult science fiction novels such as *House of Stairs, Singularity, Interstellar Pig, The Boy Who Reversed Himself,* and *Strange Attractors.* His works are consistently honored as "Best Book" selections by the American Library Association. Growing up in a suburb of St. Louis, Sleator was always writing or composing something musical and was fascinated by the grotesque and macabre. While everyone else in his family became a scientist, Sleator chose to major in English at Harvard. Following a year in England to study musical composition, he worked as a rehearsal pianist with the Boston Ballet, touring with them for nine years throughout Europe and the United States.

Sleator now lives in Boston and devotes himself to writing. He likes to write science fiction because he can learn about black holes, time travel, and chaos, and then turn these scientific phenomena into stories that have some basis in reality.

Booktalk

Have you ever wished you could be two places at once? When David discovers a mysterious machine that makes copies of living things, he thinks his wish has been answered. By duplicating himself, he reasons that he can now go to his grandma's birthday dinner, which is what his parents want him to do, and also keep his date with Angela, which is what he wants to do. While the other David is in school, the real David can spend the day at the beach. The possibilities seem endless. What freedom!

But wait. If one of them is at school, the other can't really hang around the house without being caught by David's mother, who is at home all day. David doesn't think it's a good idea to tell his parents he has duplicated himself. Would you? Just coordinating their arrivals and departures at home will take very careful planning. And food . . . only one can show up at meals. Those problems can be solved *if* David's duplicate will cooperate. But the duplicate has a mind, ideas, and desires of his own.

So what began as a solution to David's desire to be in two places at once turns into a nightmare. A terrifying nightmare. Imagine discovering that your duplicate wants you out of the way—permanently! Sign up for *The Duplicate*. Get your "copy" of this READ 'n' FEED novel before it's too late.

What's Cookin' at the READ 'n' FEED?

This science fiction novel begins on a humorous note, as the narrator muses that his life might be less complicated if there are "two of him," but it quickly turns into anything but funny. Students discuss the implications and problems of cloning and the results of impulsive behavior as they play a card game called "Multiplicity." (The rules and play are similar to the card game "Go Fish.") The object of the game is to be the first one to duplicate four cards in a hand. Play begins as a student (the original) describes to another student (the duplicate) the person, place, or thing appearing on one of his cards. The student must describe, without naming, the term. If the duplicate passes a correct clone card to the original, the original may lay down the set. If the duplicate does not have a clone, then the original must draw a GET DUPED card. A group discussion follows according to the directions on the card. In addition to the "Multiplicity" game, students explore identities in a short role-play, which follows "The Dating Game" format. Decorations, which can include goldfish as prizes for winning the "Multiplicity" game, add to this READ 'n' FEED experience.

Preparations

Refer back to "The Recipe for a Successful READ 'n' FEED Program" at the beginning of this book for a discussion of those materials, designs, resources, and handouts needed for every READ 'n' FEED. Be sure to copy the Planning Outline and Program Checklist form in the appendix of this book, so you will have it ready for your first design team meeting. In addition, *The Duplicate* program requires that you create the items needed for a card game and design a "Dating Game"-type performance area.

SHOPPING LIST

- Construction paper: lime green, light blue, yellow
- Table coverings, plates, napkins, cups, dinnerware as needed
- Goldfish bowls, goldfish, quart-size sealable bags
- Materials for a "Dating Game"-type studio set: bar stools, freestanding partition
- Materials for decorations, as suggested in the "Whipping Up the Fun" section of this chapter

ADDING THE GARNISHES

- *Authors and Artists for Young Adults.* Detroit, MI: Gales Research, 1989– .
- *Current Biography Yearbook.* New York: H. W. Wilson, 1940– .
- Trelease, Jim, ed. *Read All About It!* New York: Penguin Books, 1993.

FOOD FOR THOUGHT

Plan a menu. Because getting food to either David or the duplicate was a major problem in the novel, many selections were mentioned. Pizza, fish and chips, chocolate birthday cake, hamburgers, French fries, popcorn, steak, scalloped potatoes, French toast, and sausage are examples. Serving gingerbread men for dessert might be a creative way to carry out the duplicating theme.

WHIPPING UP THE FUN

Publicize the program. Copy the publicity poster (Template 3.1) and the Flush Flash (Template 3.2). Add local event details before displaying these promotional templates. Write a student announcement using the sample from the "Booktalk" section of this chapter. Distribute books to the students with a schedule of event dates and expectation deadlines. (See the sample Student Time Line Memo in the appendix at the end of the book.)

Select facilitators and give each of them a copy of the novel to read. At least a week before the program, supply the facilitators with any special instructions and the "Multiplicity" game rules, terms, questions, and pictures.

Find portraits of nine famous people whom your students will recognize, such as professional athletes, U.S. presidents, musicians, film and television actors, local personalities, or politicians. *Current Biography, Authors and Artists for Young Adults, People Magazine,* encyclopedias, and vertical files are good sources for pictures. Reduce or enlarge these photos on the copy machine to fit in the grid boxes for the GET DUPED picture clone cards (Template 3.8). Mount the pictures onto the grid.

Prepare one set of game cards for each discussion table. One set consists of a deck of 36 "Multiplicity" game term cards and a deck of 18 GET DUPED cards. To make the decks of cards, copy the "Multiplicity" game card backs (Template 3.4) onto one side of four sheets of lime green construction paper and two sheets of light blue construction paper. Be sure to trim the width of the construction paper to equal the width of the original copy before making these copies. Copy the "Multiplicity" game terms (Template 3.5) on the blank side of two of the green sheets. Copy more "Multiplicity" game terms (Template 3.6) on the blank side of the other two green sheets. Copy the GET DUPED questions (Template 3.7) on the blank side of one blue sheet and the GET DUPED picture grid (Template 3.8) on the other blue sheet.

Plan and prepare decorations to duplicate one of the settings in the novel. Set the mood for the army watchtower with props such as ladders, oil lamps, flashlights, buckets, brooms, cement blocks, and sleeping bags. Re-create a math classroom. Design a beach in October setting with the sounds of ocean and sea gulls from nature tapes, driftwood, sand, and shells. Or plan a birthday party for David's grandmother, complete with party favors, balloons, banners, streamers, and gift packages.

Design a simple "Dating Game" program set with four stools and a freestanding divider. You can also adapt a portable bulletin board or a large appliance box for use as a divider. It is best to try to arrange the set so that Angela cannot see the contestants.

Duplicate copies of the "Dating Game" script (Template 3.9) so you can clip apart the appropriate dialogues for the role players. From your list of participants, select one girl and three boys to act out the script and designate a facilitator to ad lib the part of the game show host. Meet separately with the girl, the host, and the boys two days before the event to explain the game format and to give each role player that part of the script that pertains to him or her. The left column on Template 3.9 is Angela's script. Trim all of Angela's questions to Contestant Three and the corresponding answer starters in the right column for David's script. Perform the same surgery on Template 3.9 to create scripts for Duplicate A and Duplicate B. (Those selected to role-play must not identify themselves to the other participants nor view each other's script.) Students should be prepared to respond to questions as their character would.

Look in magazines, encyclopedias, clip art books, or coloring books for a simple outline of a fish. With a wide tip marker place a black mark behind the gill on your fish pattern. Duplicate your pattern on yellow construction paper to make three marked duplicate fish per table for the "Multiplicity" game.

Design invitations to reflect the theme carried out by your decorations, or use the one provided with this chapter (Template 3.3). If you prefer, create an invitation to the grandmother's birthday party or prepare a secret note from David to the participant asking the student to meet David at the watchtower or the beach. Deliver these invitations the day before the program.

Plan an agenda for the day of the READ 'n' FEED. Set aside 10 minutes for the role-play, five minutes to give instructions for the "Multiplicity" game activity, and at least 25 minutes to play "Multiplicity."

Assemble the facilitators' packets. Each packet should include a place card with the facilitator's name; a copy of the novel; the Agenda and Activity Instructions with the "Multiplicity" game rules; three, yellow marked duplicate fish; and a thank-you note. Place a packet at each table.

Whetting Their Appetite

Select one of these three program ideas to prepare your students for *The Duplicate*.

- Rehearse a story to tell about William Sleator's family and childhood, using the background information on Sleator found in Jim Trelease's *Read All About It!* Read aloud "The Elevator," a short story by Sleator appearing in the same handbook.

- Invite two or three sets of twins to participate in a panel discussion of how they are alike and how they are different, and whether they think alike, do everything together, and ever get jealous of each other.

- Booktalk several other science fiction novels by William Sleator.

Mixing the Fiction, Food, and Fun

The "Dating Game" role-play starts as soon as all the students are seated. The activity follows the TV game show format. The show's host introduces Angela and the contestants, and then "Angela" quizzes "David," "Duplicate A," and "Duplicate B" before selecting one of them as her date. The host serves only as a moderator to keep the questioning and responses going. The host calls time and asks Angela to decide which contestant will be her date for the READ 'n' FEED. The audience can try to influence Angela's decision by cheering for their favorite "David" as the host says, "Will it be Contestant Number 1?" or "Contestant Number 2?" or "Contestant Number 3?" Template 3.9 provides a script guide with questions for Angela to ask and ideas for the contestants to include in their answers.

Begin the "Multiplicity" game. Play with five or six students at each table. The facilitator may need to briefly define the terms *clone, impulsive, personality traits,* and *dupe* before beginning. The object of the game is to be the first player to duplicate four cards in his or her hand!

The facilitator deals a card to each player until all 36 of the green "Multiplicity" cards are dealt. Blue GET DUPED cards are shuffled and placed in the center of table. Play begins with the player to the left of the facilitator. This original player selects a card in his or her hand and tries to find its clone by describing to a duplicate player a situation, connection, characteristic, or event from the novel that relates to the word on the card. Example: Ann asks Jim, "I would like to duplicate (description of the term). Can you help me?"

The duplicate player must pass what he or she thinks is the clone card for the person, place, or thing being described by the original player. (The duplicate is not obliged to pass any card if the description is not accurate and complete enough to determine a clone.) If the card is indeed the clone, the original player says, "Duplicate!" and lays down the pair. The original player can also lay down any other pairs in his or her hand at this time.

If the original player says the specific term on his "Multiplicity" card instead of describing the word, he or she loses a turn. The facilitator passes a marked duplicate fish to that person as a reminder of the loss of turn.

Play proceeds to the left with a new original player trying to duplicate a card in his or her hand.

If the duplicate player does not have the clone, he or she says to the original player, "Get duped!" The original player must then draw a GET DUPED card from the middle of the table.

There are two kinds of GET DUPED cards.

1. Discussion questions. The facilitator reads the question on the card that the *original* player draws and asks the group to discuss the GET DUPED question.

2. Clone pictures. The original player shows the group the picture on the card. He or she then discusses the benefits, dangers, or complications that could come from duplicating this person.

Play continues. The first person to lay down four duplicate sets is the winner. If time runs out before anyone gets four duplicates, then the player with the most duplicates wins.

Hints for a Gourmet READ 'n' FEED

Set up a simple database report to make it easier for you to verify student participation and attendance, student homerooms, book circulation, and student testing results.

Carry out the duplicating theme in the menu, decorations, and publicity. For example, place two goldfish at each table, serve two of the same sandwich, ask facilitators to dress the same, seat students by locating the duplicates of meal ticket numbers, or use a "copy" stamp to mark all invitations, agendas, and other promotional materials.

Manage your seating arrangement by giving students a number card as they check in and instruct them to find its "duplicate," which you have placed at one of the tables.

Use the manual feed function on your copy machine to duplicate the templates for the card sets. Careful planning of the placement of the original copies of the templates on the copy machine and the direction in which the construction paper is fed into the copy machine will ensure successful replication of the deck of cards. You may want to enlarge each template before duplicating it on construction paper so that the decks of cards more closely resemble the size of regular cards. Each template must be enlarged by the same percentage. Make sure the template is centered on the page before duplicating.

Review the rules for the "Multiplicity" game with students and facilitators before beginning this activity. Note that "the duplicate" and "Duplicate A" refer to the same clone.

Use the goldfish as prizes for the winners of the "Multiplicity" game. Carefully packaging each fish in a sealable bag with water will protect the fish and allow the students to take their prizes home.

Don't forget to evaluate your program. Student and facilitator comments will help you revise future programs. A sample evaluation form is included in the appendix at the end of this book.

Novel Connections

Select one or more of these follow-up activities to extend the READ 'n' FEED program:

- Show the video *Multiplicity* (Columbia Pictures, 1996; 117 min., PG13) or *Jurassic Park* (Universal City Studios, 1993; 127 minutes, PG13).

- Arrange a teleconference with a genetic scientist.

- Conduct a student opinion poll on the ethics of cloning human beings.

- Research how scientists cloned the sheep Dolly.

More Book Bites

Cooper, Margaret C. *Code Name, Clone.* New York: Walker, 1982.

Crichton, Michael. *Jurassic Park.* New York: Ballantine, 1991.

Griffith, Helen V. *Journal of a Teenage Genius.* Mahwah, NJ: Troll, 1988.

Vande Velde, Vivian. *User Unfriendly.* San Diego: Harcourt Brace Jovanovich, 1991.

Wu, William. *Hong on the Range.* New York: Walker, 1989.

Templates

Publicity Poster, Template 3.1

Flush Flash, Template 3.2

Student Invitation, Template 3.3

"Multiplicity" Game Card Backs, Template 3.4

"Multiplicity" Game Terms, Template 3.5

More "Multiplicity" Game Terms, Template 3.6

GET DUPED Questions, Template 3.7

Grid for GET DUPED Pictures, Template 3.8

Script Guide for "The Dating Game," Template 3.9

Agenda and Activity Instructions, Template 3.10

READ 'N' FEED

FICTION:

The Duplicate.
by William Sleator

WHEN:

Date:_____

Time:_____

FOOD:

SIGN-UP:

Date:_____

Where:_____

_____

FUN:

Watch your fun multiply as you GET DUPED! and "fish" for a clone.

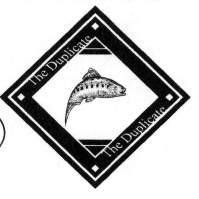

Listen to announcements for further details.

Template 3.1. Publicity Poster.

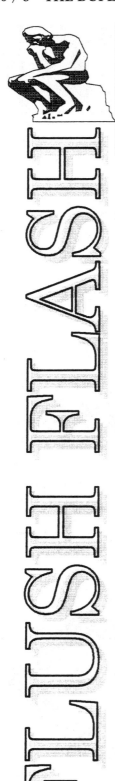

FLUSH FLASH

The Duplicate

The Duplicate

by William Sleator

Date:

Someone is trying to kill David. Is it possible that this someone is his clone? It's hard to believe that his duplicate would actually want him dead. But then the duplicate is a machine-made copy of a person. You will want to read this month's READ 'n' FEED novel, *The Duplicate*, to find out what happens to David.

"Hansel and Gretel" games

William Sleator's dad used to play a weekend game with the author and his siblings called "Hansel and Gretel." He would blindfold the kids, put them in the car, and drive them to an unknown part of the city. Then he'd take their blindfolds off and drive away, leaving them to find their way home alone.

Did they ever get lost? Maybe, but they always had a quarter to call home for help.

Bet you can't **duplicate** this joke!
"How was that science fiction movie you saw?"
"You know, same old thing—boy meets girl—boy loses girl—boy builds new girl."

Amazing clones

Scottish scientists were the first to successfully clone an adult mammal. The clone was a sheep named Dolly!

Should we copy human DNA? What do you think?

Sponsored by

Template 3.2. Flush Flash.

From *Fiction, Food, and Fun.* © 1998. Closter, Sipes, Thomas. Libraries Unlimited. (800) 237-6124.

David's
Auction Gallery

123 Oceanfront Drive

_____
(City, State)

PUBLIC AUCTION
You're Invited!

Date_____

Time_____

Place_____

SPEE-DEE-DUPE
Unique antique box
Whole machine about size of
portable television, slightly
charred exterior, shows signs of
weathering from saltwater

Not for young children. Can be
harmful. Beware of dull pop,
followed by bright flashes of light
from the lens area.

Auctioneer

_____
(Student's name)
10-5, M-F   1-800-REPLICA

Template 3.3. Student Invitation.

Template 3.4. "Multiplicity" Game Card Backs.

BOOBY
TRAP

OIL
LAMP

LADDER

BIFURCATE

BLACK
MARKS

SELF-DESTRUCT
MECHANISM

BAND
PRACTICE

SKIPPING
SCHOOL

LIFE IS HARD.
THEN YOU DIE.

Template 3.5. "Multiplicity" Game Terms.

From *Fiction, Food, and Fun.* © 1998. Closter, Sipes, Thomas. Libraries Unlimited. (800) 237-6124.

ANGELA   CARL   DAVID

DUPLICATE A   DUPLICATE B   SPEE-DEE-DUPE

TROPICAL   ARMY   POST-
FISH   WATCHTOWER   HYPNOTIC
                                        SUGGESTION

Template 3.6. More "Multiplicity" Game Terms.

GET DUPED

The duplicating machine was named SPEE-DEE-DUPE. What does the word dupe mean? Discuss how David, the duplicate, and Duplicate B were all "duped" in this novel.

GET DUPED

Review how well you liked or disliked this novel. Was the scientific issue of human cloning made believable in the story? Will you read another science fiction book by William Sleator?

GET DUPED

Thinking about the way in which the SPEE-DEE-DUPE machine was disposed, do you think the author could write a sequel to this novel? How might it begin? What kinds of characters might be involved?

GET DUPED

Give some examples of impulsive behavior. How did impulsive behavior get David into serious trouble?

GET DUPED

Describe the kinds of problems that David and the duplicate had right away. How did they seem to resolve them? How did they both try to trick and deceive each other?

GET DUPED

What motivated the duplicate to make Duplicate B? If Duplicate B had not been created, how might the novel have taken a different turn?

GET DUPED

What negative and positive personality traits did David and the duplicate have? What kind of personality did Duplicate B have?

GET DUPED

Discuss the significance of what happened to the fish that David duplicated. What insights did the fish give him to the flaws of his plan, as well as the flaws in the duplicating machine?

GET DUPED

Describe what happens at the end of the novel. How did Duplicate B contribute to his own undoing?

Template 3.7. GET DUPED Questions.

From *Fiction, Food, and Fun.* © 1998. Closter, Sipes, Thomas. Libraries Unlimited. (800) 237-6124.

Template 3.8. Grid for GET DUPED Pictures.

Questions **ANGELA**	Answers starters for **DAVID (3), DUPLICATE A (2), DUPLICATE B (1)**
Contestant 3, convince me that you are better looking than the other two contestants.	DAVID (3): Good looking; nice tan; no birthmarks
Contestant 2, the same question.	DUPLICATE A (2): Blond; look like the other two, only more handsome
Contestant 3, when you first discovered the SPEE-DEE-DUPE, what did you think it was?	DAVID (3): Had no idea but thought it might be some type of experimental device
Contestant 1, what did you think it was?	DUPLICATE B (1): Knew it was a duplicating machine; something that I could use to my advantage
Contestant 2, if I choose you to go on the big date, what will we do?	DUPLICATE A (2): Order a pizza; sit around your house and talk
Contestant 3, what will we do on our date?	DAVID (3): Go to the beach; eat all the junk food we want; go to a movie
Contestant 1, would you consider yourself to be trustworthy?	DUPLICATE B (1): Sure, but most people think I'm artificial
Contestant 2, how will I know that you are a guy who can be trusted?	DUPLICATE A (2): Helped a friend out who was in serious trouble; keep my promises
Contestant 3, what is the most exciting thing you have ever done?	DAVID (3): Be in two places at once
Contestant 1, have you ever done anything real exciting?	DUPLICATE B (1): Camped out all night by myself in a deserted watchtower
Contestant 2, is there any reason why I should pick you instead of one of the other contestants to take me out?	DUPLICATE A (2) Tough; brave; a "take charge" kind of person
Contestant 3, why should I pick you?	DAVID (3): Smarter; skilled at posthypnotic suggestion, so you'll think we are together all the time; good kisser; other contestants are menaces, just biological robots
Contestant 1, why should you be my date?	DUPLICATE B (1) : Clever; strong; more experienced

Template 3.9. Script Guide for "The Dating Game."

READ 'n' FEED
The Duplicate
Agenda

_____	(10 min.)	Serve and seat participants; begin eating
_____	(10 min.)	"Dating Game" role-play
_____	(5 min.)	Activity instructions
_____	(25 min.)	Play "Multiplicity"
_____	(5 min.)	Award prizes to winners and clean up

Activity Instructions

MULTIPLICITY

Object of the game: Be the first to duplicate four cards in your hand!

Players: 5 to 6 students

*Facilitator: "Multiplicity" is a game similar to the children's card game "Go Fish."
You may need to briefly define the terms* clone, impulsive, personality traits, *and* dupe
*before beginning. Shuffle the blue and the green decks of cards. Deal out all green
"Multiplicity" cards to players. Place blue* **GET DUPED** *cards in the center of the
table. If there are only five students at your table, you may elect to play the game also.*

Play begins with the player to the left of the facilitator. This original player selects a
card in his or her hand and tries to find its clone by describing to a duplicate player a
situation, connection, characteristic, or event from the novel that relates to the word on
the card. Example: Ann asks Jim, "I would like to duplicate <u>(description of the term on
the "Multiplicity" card)</u>. Can you help me?"

The duplicate player must pass what he or she thinks is the clone card for the person,
place, or thing being described by the original player.   If the card passed is the clone,
the original player says, "Duplicate!" and lays down the pair. The original player can
also lay down any other pairs in his or her hand at this time.

*Facilitator: If a player says the specific term on his "Multiplicity" card instead of
describing the word, he or she loses a turn. Pass a marked duplicate fish to that player
as a reminder of the loss of turn. Explain that the duplicate player is not obliged to
pass any card if the description is not accurate and complete enough to determine a
clone.*

Play proceeds to the left with a new original player trying to duplicate a card in his or
her hand. If the duplicate player does not have the clone, he or she says to the
original player, "Get duped!" The original player must then draw a GET DUPED card
from the middle of the table.

Facilitator: There are two kinds of **GET DUPED** *cards.*

*1. Discussion questions. Read aloud the question on the card that the original player
draws and ask the group to discuss the* **GET DUPED** *question.*

*2. Clone pictures. The original player shows the group the picture on the card. Ask
him or her to discuss the benefits, dangers, or complications of duplicating this person.*

Play continues. The first person to lay down four duplicate sets is the winner. If time
runs out before anyone gets four duplicates, the player with the most duplicates wins.

Template 3.10. Agenda and Activity Instructions.

From *Fiction, Food, and Fun.* © 1998. Closter, Sipes, Thomas. Libraries Unlimited. (800) 237-6124.

Chapter **4**

Fallen Angels

Bibliographic Information

Walter Dean Myers. *Fallen Angels*. New York: Scholastic, 1988. 309 pages. $3.95. ISBN 0-590-40943-3.

Interest Level

Grades 8 through 12

Themes

War, Life and Death, Survival, Compassion, Initiation (loss of innocence)

Plot Summary

Upon graduation from high school in the New York Bronx, Richie Perry's visions of going to college, becoming a writer, and playing basketball for the U.S. Army disappear when he is shipped out to Vietnam. It is 1967. Richie is a foot soldier near the demilitarized zone (DMZ) where it is difficult to distinguish just who and where the enemy is.

Author Information

Walter Dean Myers grew up in Harlem in the home of foster parents. Perhaps due to a speech impediment, written expression came easy to him. He learned to enjoy reading, composing poetry, and writing stories. Adolescence proved to be turbulent, and in 1954, he quit school and joined the army. He worked at various jobs, continuing his writing, until one of his stories won a contest. His writing since then has been nothing less than prolific as well as award winning. *Fallen Angels* was the recipient of the 1989 Coretta Scott King award, the 1988 ALA Best Books for Young Adults award, and the 1988 *School Library Journal* Best Book award.

Booktalk

Richie had everything planned. There was no way his mother could afford college, but if he enlisted, the U.S. Army would pay for his education. He could play basketball and continue to write, all while doing his duty and serving his country. But it is 1967. The Vietnam War is raging, and soon he finds himself in the middle of a steaming jungle trying to stay alive so he can get back to "The World" with his brother and mom. He lives through hours of monotony and seconds of terror. He watches, helplessly, as many of his friends are zipped into body bags. One wrong move and he, too, will have no more stories to tell.

What's Cookin' at the READ 'n' FEED?

This is a powerful novel about war and its effects on people. Students enter a military camp atmosphere with dog tags as their passes. Vietnam veterans serve as squadron leaders at each table. The activities are fast-paced to create a sense of immediacy and uncertainty. Only five minutes are allotted to complete orders at each table at which time a whistle blows, signaling a change of station. The guest veterans field questions for the final activity.

Preparations

Read "The Recipe for a Successful READ 'n' FEED Program" at the beginning of this book for a discussion of those materials, designs, resources, and handouts needed for every READ 'n' FEED. Be sure to copy the Planning Outline and Program Checklist form in the appendix of this book, so you will have it ready for your first design meeting.

In addition, this program requires squad orders for each table. Invite local Vietnam veterans to participate as facilitators; check local directories for listings of AMVET organizations in your community. Ask an Army-Navy surplus store to make dog tags for all participants saying "Reader First Class" and bearing the names of the students.

SHOPPING LIST

- Table coverings, plates, napkins, cups, dinnerware as needed
- Materials for decorations—military equipment, uniforms, army blankets, cots, combat boots, photographs of Vietnam, and other military-inspired items
- Construction paper in jungle camouflage colors: black, green, tan, brown
- Candy that looks like peas and carrots
- Pencils
- Dog tags
- Helmets or small buckets

ADDING THE GARNISHES

- Allen, Thomas B. *Offerings at the Wall: Artifacts from the Vietnam Veterans Memorial Collection*. Atlanta, GA: Turner Publishing, 1995.

- AMVETS National Headquarters, 4647 Forbes Boulevard, Lanham, MD 20706-4380, (301) 459-9600; Web site: http://www.amvets.org./

- Bunting, Eve. *The Wall.* Illus. by Ronald Himler. New York: Clarion Books, 1990.

- Friends of the Vietnam Veterans Memorial, 2030 Clarendon Boulevard, Suite 412, Arlington, VA 22201, (703) 525-1107.

- Moser, Don. "Offerings at the Wall." *Smithsonian* 26(2) (May 1995): 54–59. This article summarizes the book, *Offerings at the Wall* by Allen.

- "Offerings at the Wall" cyberarticle at http://photo2.si.edu/offerings/offerings.html

- The Vietnam Veterans Memorial Wall homepage at http://www.thewall-usa.com/index.html

FOOD FOR THOUGHT

Food is mentioned often in *Fallen Angels.* Incorporate into your menu several of the foods mentioned such as roast beef, mashed potatoes, peas, carrots, carrot cake, chocolate bars, caramels, and orange Jello. Borrow cafeteria trays to enhance the mess hall atmosphere and to make it easier for the participants to transfer from station to station during the meal.

WHIPPING UP THE FUN

Publicize the program. Copy the publicity poster (Template 4.1) and the Flush Flash (Template 4.2). Add local event details before displaying these promotional templates. Write a student announcement using the sample from the "Booktalk" section of this chapter. Distribute books to the students with a schedule of event dates and expectation deadlines. (See the sample Student Time Line Memo in the appendix at the end of this book.)

Select facilitators and give each of them a copy of the novel to read. At least a week before the program, supply the facilitators with any special instructions and the Agenda and Activity Instructions (Template 4.4).

Divide the number of students who will be participating by five; run that many copies of the red, blue, green, white, and black squad orders (Templates 4.5–4.9). Collate these so that equal numbers of students will rotate among each station.

Reproduce two copies of each sign (Templates 4.10–4.14) for the tables. Sandwich a piece of construction paper between the backs of the two copies to frame them and make them rigid enough to stand alone.

Copy enough of Templates 4.15 through 4.19 for each participant, making sure to keep all of the orders on the correct tables. For example, all of the Chu Lai Orders (Template 4.15) belong on the table with the Chu Lai table sign (Template 4.10). If you are able to find helmets for each table, place the orders in the helmets. Otherwise, use a metal bucket to hold the orders.

Assemble the facilitators' packets. Include a place card with the facilitator's name, a copy of the novel, and the Agenda and Activity Instructions (Template 4.4), and a thank-you note. Some tables will need specific items. For example, the Tam Ky table will need *Offerings at the Wall* (Turner, 1995) or another available source of information about the Vietnam War Memorial.

Whetting Their Appetite

Select one of these program ideas to prepare your students for *Fallen Angels*.

- Read aloud the picture book *The Wall* by Eve Bunting.

- Show video clips from Vietnam War coverage.

- Invite a psychologist who works with veterans to make a short presentation about post-traumatic stress syndrome.

Mixing the Fiction, Food, and Fun

A few minutes before the students arrive, the squadron leaders (discussion leaders or facilitators) are served their food trays at their assigned table. As troops (students) enter, they are handed their color squad orders, one of Templates 4.5 through 4.9. Their first order is to go through the mess line. The second order tells them which table to go to. Orders are completed quickly with only five minutes at a station. When the signal is given, the color squads transfer to their new stations. The facilitators remain at the same table throughout the READ 'n' FEED program. They are responsible for overseeing one set of orders for each set of troops that rotates to the table. The agenda and activity instructions, Template 4.4, detail the tours of duty. Chu Lai orders are to write a letter to the family of a friend killed by friendly fire. How do you tell them that their son was killed by their fellow troops? Ft. Devens orders are to match the characters from the book with their descriptions. Explain which leader you would rather have. Tam Ky orders are to make a list of items that you would place at the Vietnam War Memorial in memory of a loved one who died in the war. Quang Nam orders are to plan a cybervisit to The Wall at http://www.thewall-usa.com by writing a message to the Vietnam Veterans of America at this site. Students write their message on the orders provided so that they will be ready to sign the guest book when they access the Internet at a later time. The World orders are to write questions that you would like the Vietnam Veterans who are visiting to answer during the last activity.

Hints for a Gourmet READ 'n' FEED

Set up a simple database to make it easier for you to verify student participation and attendance, student homerooms, book circulation, and student testing results.

Allow at least 45 minutes to complete this READ 'n' FEED. Ask for parent or teacher volunteers to serve the food dressed in fatigues.

Invite Vietnam veterans, local university instructors, or psychologists who specialize in the Vietnam era to attend. Including Vietnam veterans in this activity is strongly recommended because they add a dimension to the program that could not otherwise be achieved. The following three correspondences attest to this and show the mutual benefits that result when students interact with veterans. The first letter is from a student thanking one of the veterans for coming. The second and third letters are from the veteran who received the letter.

Dear Mr. Hiatt, I wish to thank you for coming and telling us about your Vietnam experiences in our monthly READ 'n' FEED. It was a real nice thing that you did, just by coming. After reading the book *Fallen Angels* and listening to you all talk about the war, it gave me a better understanding of what you went through in Vietnam. I think that it must have been hard to not be able to have real close friends. I know it must have been hard for you to share your memories of the war. We all appreciate what you did to help our READ 'n' FEED program and what you've done to help our country. Sincerely, Christy Mains

Dear Christy, I got your letter to William Hiatt by mistake. I wanted to take this time to thank you and your friends for giving me back a lot of pride. I too am a Vietnam veteran. Speaking for all Vietnam veterans, with you and your classmates as our future leaders, I doubt there will ever be a war like that again. My most sincere thanks, Michael Hyatt (Vietnam 1970–71)

P.S. I went to South Side myself—many years ago!

Dear Sir, I received a letter by mistake from a student of yours. The letter was intended for a William Hiatt at this address. I am returning the letter for forwarding to the right Mr. Hiatt. (Please note spelling of last name.)

It was very ironic—for I, too, am a Vietnam veteran. The letter was very touching and heartwarming for me. If possible could you please forward the enclosed letter from me to a Miss Christy Mains. Thank you, Michael Hyatt

Don't forget to evaluate your program. Students and facilitator comments will help you revise and adjust future READ 'n' FEED programs. A sample evaluation form is included in the appendix at the end of this book.

Novel Connections

Select one or more of these follow-up activities to extend the READ 'n' FEED program:

- Students sign the Vietnam Veterans Memorial Wall Page guest book (http://www.cpeg.com/~wall/guestbook/guestbook.html) and leave the message they prepared in their Quang Nam orders.

- Encourage students to organize a fund-raising drive for local veteran post.

- Help students plan a program to commemorate Veteran's Day or Memorial Day.

- Plan a field trip to visit a war memorial in the vicinity.

- Invite students to write a poem or essay dedicated to the veterans of war.

More Book Bites

Amos, James. *The Memorial: A Novel of the Vietnam War.* New York: Crown, 1989.

Baklanov, Grigory. *Forever Nineteen.* New York: Lippincott, 1989.

Emerson, Zack. *Hill 568.* New York: Scholastic, 1991.

Hahn, Mary Downing. *December Stillness.* New York: Clarion Books, 1988.

Jensen, Kathryn. *Pocket Change.* New York: Macmillan, 1989.

Mason, Bobbie Ann. *In Country: A Novel.* New York: Harper & Row, 1985.

Mazer, Harry. *The Last Mission.* New York: Delacorte Press, 1979.

Nelson, Theresa. *And One for All.* New York: Orchard Books, 1989.

Noonan, Michael. *McKenzie's Boots*. New York: Orchard Books, 1988.

O'Brien, Tim. *The Things They Carried*. Franklin Center, PA: Franklin Library, 1990.

Remarque, Erich Marie. *All Quiet on the Western Front*. New York: Bantam, 1985.

Rostkowski, Margaret I. *The Best of Friends*. New York: Harper & Row, 1989.

Templates

Publicity Poster, Template 4.1

Flush Flash, Template 4.2

Invitation, Template 4.3

Agenda and Activity Instructions, Template 4.4

Red Squad Orders, Template 4.5

Blue Squad Orders, Template 4.6

Green Squad Orders, Template 4.7

White Squad Orders, Template 4.8

Black Squad Orders, Template 4.9

Chu Lai Table Sign, Template 4.10

Ft. Devens Table Sign, Template 4.11

Tam Ky Table Sign, Template 4.12

Quang Nam Table Sign, Template 4.13

The World Table Sign, Template 4.14

Chu Lai Orders, Template 4.15

Ft. Devens Orders, Template 4.16

Tam Ky Orders, Template 4.17

Quang Nam Orders, Template 4.18

The World Orders, Template 4.19

READ 'n' FEED WANTS YOU!

*Fallen Angels**

by
Walter
Dean
Myers

★ _____ ★

Where   When

We're looking for a few good persons . Check it out in the library!
*Parent permission slip may be required due to strong language.

Template 4.1. Publicity Poster.

FALLEN ANGELS

Date:

by Walter Dean Myers

Walter Dean Myers dedicated his book *Fallen Angels* to his brother, Thomas Wayne "Sonny" Myers, who died in Vietnam in 1968. Sonny was one of more than 58,000 soldiers who were killed in that war.

Walter Dean Myers wrote stories when he was a boy. Writing and basketball were his hobbies. One of his latest books, *Slam*, is about a kid who goes through a lot of changes in a short time, including moving to a different school and playing on the basketball team.

Check it out!

The Wall

The first memento to be placed at the Vietnam War Memorial was by a soldier whose brother had been killed in Vietnam. He tossed his brother's Purple Heart Medal of Honor into the still wet cement at the base of the Wall where his brother's name was. Since then, thousands of mementoes have been placed there by loved ones.

Sponsored by

Template 4.2. Flush Flash.

From *Fiction, Food, and Fun.* © 1998. Closter, Sipes, Thomas. Libraries Unlimited. (800) 237-6124.

To: Reader First Class

_____ :

You have successfully passed
the preliminary requirements
for induction into the
U.S.R.F.P.*

Your orders are to report:

to
_____
at   hours
with these orders in hand.

*UNITED STATES READ 'N' FEED PROGRAM

READ 'n' FEED
WANTS
YOU!!!!

Fallen Angels

by Walter Dean Myers

Template 4.3. Invitation.

READ 'n' FEED

Fallen Angels

Agenda

_____	(5 min.)	Troops receive orders, go through mess line, and begin eating
_____	(1 min.)	Welcome
_____	(5 min.)	Station #2
_____	(5 min.)	Station #3
_____	(5 min.)	Station #4
_____	(5 min.)	Station #5
_____	(15 min.)	Vietnam veterans answer questions
_____	(1 min.)	Dismissal

Activity Instructions

Facilitators: This is a working lunch. Begin activities as soon as your group arrives at the table. You are to give the same set of orders for each group of troops.

 Squadron Tours of Duty

Red Squad: Tam Ky to Quang Nam to The World to Chu Lai to Ft. Devens
Blue Squad: Ft. Devens to Tam Ky to Quang Nam to The World to Chu Lai
Green Squad: Quang Nam to The World to Chu Lai to Ft. Devens to Tam Ky
White Squad: The World to Chu Lai to Ft. Devens to Tam Ky to Quang Nam
Black Squad: Chu Lai to Ft. Devens to Tam Ky to Quang Nam to The World

Station	Order to be Completed
Chu Lai	Write a letter to the family of one of your friends who was killed by friendly fire.
Ft. Devens	Match the characters with their descriptions. Explain which leaders you would rather have.
Tam Ky	Make a list of things that you would place at the Vietnam War Memorial in memory of those who died.
Quang Nam	Plan to make a cybervisit to The Wall. Go to http://www.thewall-usa.com and sign the guest book. Write a message to the Vietnam vets.
The World	Write questions that you would like to have our guests answer today.

Template 4.4. Agenda and Activity Instructions.

SQUAD ORDERS
RED

You have been assigned to the Red Squadron. Follow the instructions below. Do not deviate from your placement, or you could face disciplinary procedures.

Order # 1:	Get your mess tray
Order # 2:	Report to Tam Ky
Order # 3:	Complete orders at Tam Ky
Order # 4:	Transfer to Quang Nam
Order # 5:	Complete orders at Quang Nam
Order # 6:	Transfer to The World
Order # 7:	Complete orders at The World
Order # 8:	Transfer to Chu Lai
Order # 9:	Complete orders at Chu Lai
Order # 10:	Transfer to Ft. Devens
Order # 11:	Complete orders at Ft. Devens

After completing all transfers and orders, wait for further instructions from your Commanding Officers.

Template 4.5. Red Squad Orders.

From *Fiction, Food, and Fun.* © 1998. Closter, Sipes, Thomas. Libraries Unlimited. (800) 237-6124.

SQUAD ORDERS

BLUE

You have been assigned to the Blue Squadron. Follow the instructions below. Do not deviate from your placement, or you could face disciplinary procedures.

Order # 1:	Get your mess tray
Order # 2:	Report to Ft. Devens
Order # 3:	Complete orders at Ft. Devens
Order # 4:	Transfer to Tam Ky
Order # 5:	Complete orders at Tam Ky
Order # 6:	Transfer to Quang Nam
Order # 7:	Complete orders at Quang Nam
Order # 8:	Transfer to The World
Order # 9:	Complete orders at The World
Order # 10:	Transfer to Chu Lai
Order # 11:	Complete orders at Chu Lai

After completing all transfers and orders, wait for further instructions from your Commanding Officers.

Template 4.6. Blue Squad Orders.

You have been assigned to the Green Squadron. Follow the instructions below. Do not deviate from your placement, or you could face disciplinary procedures.

Order # 1:	Get your mess tray
Order # 2:	Report to Quang Nam
Order # 3:	Complete orders at Quang Nam
Order # 4:	Transfer to The World
Order # 5:	Complete orders at The World
Order # 6:	Transfer to Chu Lai
Order # 7:	Complete orders at Chu Lai
Order # 8:	Transfer to Ft. Devens
Order # 9:	Complete orders at Ft. Devens
Order # 10:	Transfer to Tam Ky
Order # 11:	Complete orders at Tam Ky

After completing all transfers and orders, wait for further instructions from your Commanding Officers.

Template 4.7. Green Squad Orders.

From *Fiction, Food, and Fun.* © 1998. Closter, Sipes, Thomas. Libraries Unlimited. (800) 237-6124.

SQUAD ORDERS

WHITE

You have been assigned to the White Squadron. Follow the instructions below. Do not deviate from your placement, or you could face disciplinary procedures.

Order # 1:	Get your mess tray
Order # 2:	Report to The World
Order # 3:	Complete orders at The World
Order # 4:	Transfer to Chu Lai
Order # 5:	Complete orders at Chu Lai
Order # 6:	Transfer to Ft. Devens
Order # 7:	Complete orders at Ft. Devens
Order # 8:	Transfer to Tam Ky
Order # 9:	Complete orders at Tam Ky
Order # 10:	Transfer to Quang Nam
Order # 11:	Complete orders at Quang Nam

After completing all transfers and orders, wait for further instructions from your Commanding Officers.

Template 4.8. White Squad Orders.

SQUAD ORDERS
BLACK

You have been assigned to the Black Squadron. Follow the instructions below. Do not deviate from your placement, or you could face disciplinary procedures.

Order # 1:	Get your mess tray
Order # 2:	Report to Chu Lai
Order # 3:	Complete orders at Chu Lai
Order # 4:	Transfer to Ft. Devens
Order # 5:	Complete orders at Ft. Devens
Order # 6:	Transfer to Tam Ky
Order # 7:	Complete orders at Tam Ky
Order # 8:	Transfer to Quang Nam
Order # 9:	Complete orders at Quang Nam
Order # 10:	Transfer to The World
Order # 11:	Complete orders at The World

After completing all transfers and orders, wait for further instructions from your Commanding Officers.

Template 4.9. Black Squad Orders.

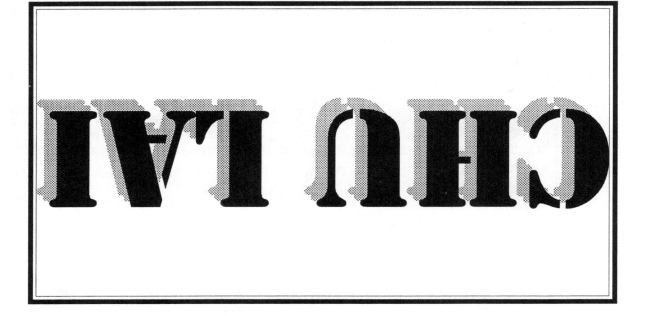

Template 4.10. Chu Lai Table Sign.

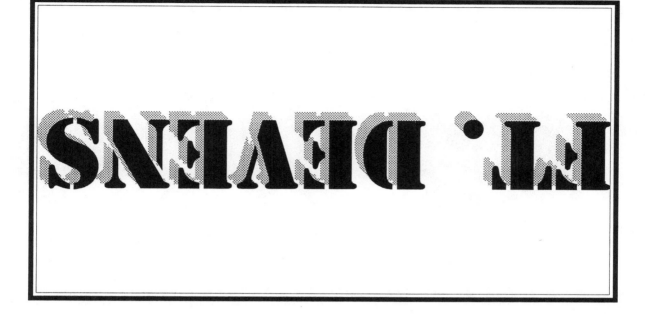

Template 4.11. Ft. Devens Table Sign.

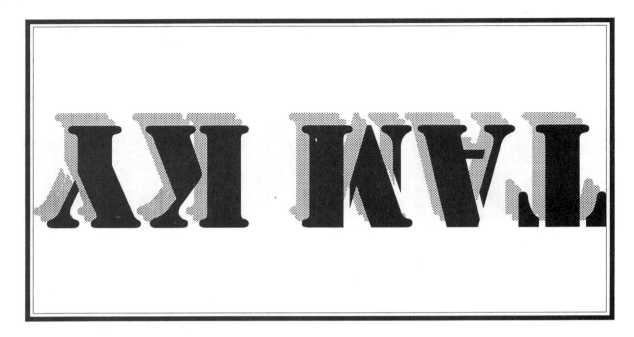

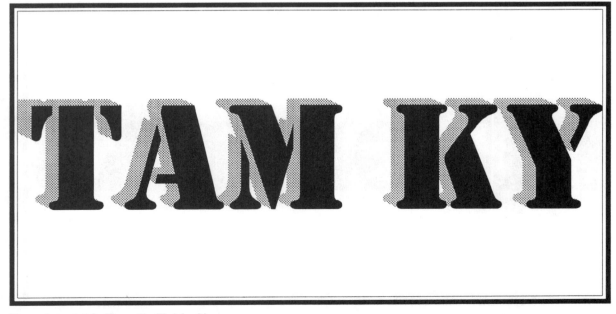

Template 4.12. Tam Ky Table Sign.

QUANG NAM

Template 4.13. Quang Nam Table Sign.

Template 4.14. The World Table Sign.

CHU LAI, VIETNAM
ORDERS

Write a letter to the closest relative of one of your squad members who died in "friendly fire." Are you going to be completely truthful in your letter? Why or why not?
Use the stationery provided below. Hand your letter to your squad leader before you report to your next location. Remember you have only a few minutes to complete this exercise, but regardless, make it a thoughtful and meaningful response.

UNITED STATES ARMED FORCES
CHU LAI, VIETNAM

Dear _____,

Sincerely yours,

Template 4.15. Chu Lai Orders.

FT. DEVENS
ORDERS

Match the characters listed with their descriptions. You may use the descriptions with more than one character. Choose which character you would rather have as a leader and why.

1. Tough guy

2. Gentle

3. Prejudiced

4. Career man

5. Battle smart

6. Experienced soldier

7. Ends up dead

8. Bends the rules

9. Follows orders

10. Tells everyone that getting out alive is his goal

_____ Lt. Carroll

_____ Capt. Stewert

_____ Lt. Gearhart

_____ Sgt. Simpson

_____ Sgt. Dongan

_____ Lt. Doyle

Which of these characters would you rather have as a leader? Why?

Template 4.16. Ft. Devens Orders.

TAM KY
ORDERS

Every year, hundreds of people leave items at "the Wall" in honor of those who died in the Vietnam War. What would you leave at the memorial if you were to visit? Use the space below for your answer.

Template 4.17. Tam Ky Orders.

QUANG NAM
ORDERS

Plan a cybervisit to the Vietnam War Memorial.
Write a message to those who served in Vietnam that will be
posted to the web site:
http://www.thewall-usa.com/index.html

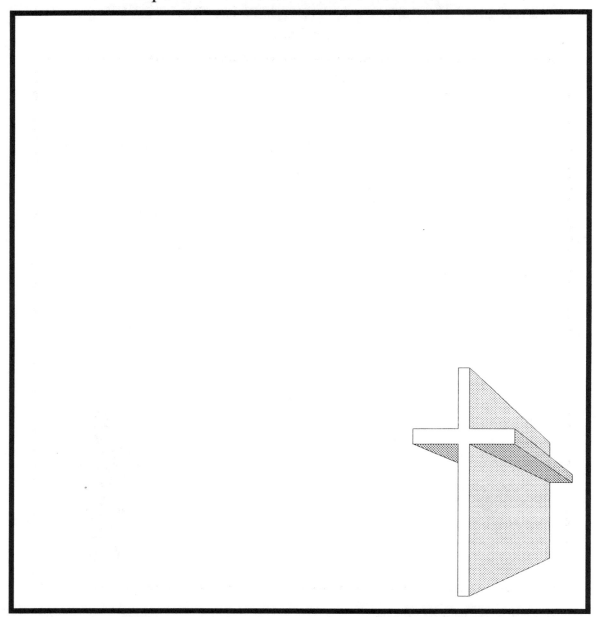

Template 4.18. Quang Nam Orders.

THE WORLD
ORDERS

In the space provided below, write questions that you would like to have our visiting Vietnam veterans answer.

Template 4.19. The World Orders.

Chapter **5**

Flight #116 Is Down

Bibliographic Information

Caroline B. Cooney. *Flight #116 Is Down.* New York: Scholastic, 1992. 201 pages. $3.99. ISBN 0-590-4479-4.

Interest Level

Grades 7 through 9

Themes

Responsibility, Life and Death, Survival, Compassion, Disaster

Plot Summary

Teenager Heidi Landseth helps with the rescue effort when a huge plane crashes on her family's property. The experience changes her life forever.

Author Information

Caroline B. Cooney lives in the seacoast town of Westbrook, Connecticut, with the youngest of her three children. She writes every day. She also walks the beach to think about what she might write next, daydreams, reads mystery novels, volunteers at a local hospital, embroiders, and plays the piano for the school musicals. She has written more than 50 books for young adults in every genre. Her special knack for holding the interest of teenage readers is apparent, whether she's writing humor, romance, suspense, or thrillers.

Booktalk

Saturday, 5:40 p.m. Everything is quiet, uninteresting, ordinary. Heidi Landseth is bored. Patrick Farquhar describes things as dull, very, very dull. Nothing ever happens in the little town of Nearing River. Saturday, 5:41 p.m. Everything is loud, explosive, violent. Heidi now tells how frightened she is. Patrick describes things as terrifying and exciting. Something big has happened. A 747 has crashed and is burning in Heidi's yard. Saturday, 5:42 p.m. Flight #116 is down! Heidi and Patrick are the first ones to arrive on the scene. Too many things are happening. There is too much noise; too many life-and-death decisions to be made. Help! *Flight #116 Is Down* by Caroline B. Cooney.

What's Cookin' at the READ 'n' FEED?

A jumbo passenger jetliner crashes in Heidi's backyard. Many survive the crash and need immediate attention. The READ 'n' FEED atmosphere is one of a massive rescue operation. Because students read the points of view of several characters in this novel, facilitators begin discussion at their tables by reading quotes from survivors of actual plane crashes. The activities revolve around a game called "TRIAGE: A Game of Rescue and Survival." This game uses a bingo-type game board and three types of questions, which represent the three stages of triage. The object of the game is to be the first player to mark all three triage colors (red, green, and yellow) in a row. Although, and perhaps because, the subject matter is very serious, some comic relief may be found in the awarding of miniature plastic body parts as prizes to the winners of the game. The mood is lightened by this kind of macabre humor which the adolescent audience seems to enjoy.

Preparations

Read "The Recipe for a Successful READ 'n' FEED Program" at the beginning of this book for a discussion of those materials, designs, resources, and handouts needed for every READ 'n' FEED. Be sure to copy the Planning Outline and Program Checklist form in the appendix of this book, so you will have it ready for your first design team meeting. *Flight #116 Is Down* offers a great opportunity to involve Red Cross volunteers and emergency medical technicians from the community. This program requires assembly of Rescue cards and game boards and locating quotes from plane crash survivors.

SHOPPING LIST

- Miniature plastic body parts (Contact: Oriental Trading Company, 800-228-2269)
- Self-adhesive name tags
- Table coverings, plates, napkins, cups, dinnerware as needed
- Materials for decoration; medical supplies, IV bags, a gurney with Resusi Annie, stethoscopes, surgical gloves, stretchers, gauze bandages, confetti glitter
- Construction paper: red, yellow, black, green, and white
- Card stock paper: red
- One-half-inch adhesive dots: red, yellow, black, and green
- Pencils

ADDING THE GARNISHES

- Red Cross personnel
- Emergency medical technicians
- *Life* magazine 12, no. 10 (September 1989): 28–32

FOOD FOR THOUGHT

Feeding the rescue workers and survivors is a problem for the housekeeper in *Flight #116 Is Down*. Plan a menu, using several foods mentioned such as donuts, chocolate bars, cole slaw, peanut butter, soup, tuna fish, bacon, coffee, and peanut snacks.

WHIPPING UP THE FUN

Publicize the program. Copy the publicity poster (Template 5.1) and the Flush Flash (Template 5.2). Add local event details before displaying these promotional templates. Write a student announcement using the sample from the "Booktalk" section of this chapter. Distribute books to the students with a schedule of event dates and expectation deadlines. (See the sample Student Time Line Memo in the appendix at the end of this book.)

Use large pieces of construction paper in yellow, green, red, black, and white as placemats. Make small circles of the same colors to place on students' nametags for seat assignments. This will allow for the even distribution of students as they enter and take their seats.

Reproduce five "TRIAGE" Game Cards (Template 5.4) for each table. Apply adhesive color dots to the game cards by following the five different color patterns shown on Template 5.4; (Y=yellow, R=red, G=green, B=black, W=white). Because no two students at a table should have the same color dot pattern, make sure each table has five different patterns. Laminate each game card.

For each table of five players, reproduce the Rescue Card Back (Template 5.5) on 9 sheets of red card stock. On the reverse side of 8 of those sheets, reproduce Rescue Card Questions (Templates 5.6a–5.6h) so that each table has a complete set of cards: 16 R (red) coded cards—thinking/feeling questions; 16 Y (yellow) coded cards—comprehension questions; and 16 G (green) coded cards—role play/research situations. On the reverse side of the remaining sheet of red card stock that you prepared, reproduce the Rescue Death Card Face, Template 5.7. You will need only two Death cards for each deck. Laminate the card sheets, then trim the cards apart to make a deck for each table of five players. It is important to keep each set of cards that you make separate so that the game plays the way it is intended.

Find quotes from plane crash survivors in magazines to use with the opening discussion activity. Enlarge the quotes and mount each on half sheets of yellow, red, green, or black construction paper. Include two or three different quotes for each table.

Select facilitators and give each of them a copy of the novel to read. One week before the program, give the facilitators the quotations from plane crash survivors, the description of how to play the game, a sample "TRIAGE" Game Card, and copies of the questions found on the Rescue Cards.

Copy the student invitation (Template 5.3) to use as admission into the READ 'n' FEED program. Address this invitation to students who qualify to attend the program.

Copy Template 5.8 to include in the facilitator's packet for each table. Also include a place card with the facilitator's name, a copy of the novel, crash survivor quote cards, and a thank-you note.

Decorate the area using medical supplies. Decorate tables with red, green, or yellow coverings or use student-designed placemats. Add confetti and miniature plastic body parts (or miniature chocolates) in the middle of each table. Each table needs six place settings; five with a "TRIAGE" game card and pencils and one with a facilitator's packet.

Whetting Their Appetite

Select one of these program ideas to prepare your students for *Flight #116 Is Down*.

- Invite emergency medical technicians to make a short presentation about the triage system.

- Ask Red Cross volunteers to explain the mission of their organization in the event of a disaster such as the one described in the book.

- Have a psychologist make a short presentation about common reactions that the families of plane crash victims exhibit.

Mixing the Fiction, Food, and Fun

To begin, the facilitators at each table read a card quoting a survivor of a plane crash. Students discuss their reactions to the person's recollection or compare the statement to dialogue among the survivors in the novel.

Introduce the Red Cross and emergency medical technician guests and explain what role they will play during the game.

Explain to students the rules for playing "TRIAGE: A Game of Rescue and Survival." "TRIAGE" is played like Bingo. The object of the game is to complete a row of four across, down, or diagonally. The player can only win with a row that includes at least one of each of the three triage colors: red, green, and yellow.

Play begins with the student to the left of the facilitator. The player draws a card from the Rescue card deck and reads the question aloud. The player must answer the question or follow the directions given on the Rescue card. Note what color the card is coded: yellow, green, or red. If the discussion leader thinks the player has fulfilled the requirements as requested on the Rescue card, he or she instructs the player to mark an *X* on one of his or her game card color dots. The player must choose a dot that matches the color at the bottom of the Rescue card he or she just played. If a player draws a Rescue card with the skull and crossbones, one row on that player's game card with the black dot in it "dies" and cannot be used to win.

Play continues to the left until a player wins by marking a row of three different triage colors: red, yellow, and green.

Hints for a Gourmet READ 'n' FEED

Set up a simple database report to make it easier for you to verify student participation and attendance, student homerooms, book circulation, and student testing results.

Plan 45 minutes to complete this READ 'n' FEED. This is a working lunch. Allow 10 minutes to serve food and begin eating; 5 minutes for the opening discussion of the quotes from plane crash survivors; and 20 minutes to play "TRIAGE: A Game of Rescue and Survival."

Use triage colors to organize the students into their discussion groups/tables.

Invite Red Cross personnel or emergency medical technicians to the activity so that they can be a resource for the role-play/research questions.

Continue to play the game until all players have the opportunity to "bingo."

Allow players to select a miniature plastic body part from the table decorations as soon as they "bingo." Know your audience! Substitute miniature chocolate candies for prizes if you think using the plastic body parts would be inappropriate.

Don't forget to evaluate your program. Students and facilitator comments will help you revise and adjust future READ 'n' FEED programs. A sample evaluation form is included in the appendix at the end of this book.

Novel Connections

Select one or more of these follow-up activities to extend the READ 'n' FEED program:

- Help students organize a food drive for a local pantry or collect donations for the Red Cross.
- Write to the National Air Disaster Alliance for information about the organization, and invite a survivor support group member to share information with the students.
- Encourage students to volunteer to work at emergency management facilities, ambulance service companies, or hospitals.

More Book Bites

Bauer, Marion Dane. *Face to Face*. New York: Clarion Books, 1991.

Blackwood, Gary L. *Wild Timothy*. New York: Atheneum, 1987.

Mayne, William. *Drift*. New York: Delacorte Press, 1986.

Paulsen, Gary. *The River*. New York: Delacorte Press, 1991.

———. *Voyage of the Frog*. New York: Orchard Books, 1989.

Ruckman, Ivy. *Night of the Twisters*. New York: Crowell, 1984.

Templates

Template 5.1. Publicity Poster.

Flight #116 Is Down

by Caroline B. Cooney

Date:

What would you do if a plane crashed in your backyard? Find out how Heidi helped with the rescue and how doing so changed her life forever.

You can experience the emotions of this disaster by signing up to read *Flight #116 Is Down*. When you read, we feed!

Sponsored by

TRIAGE?

Red, green, and yellow represent the stages of triage. The term originally referred to the method of sorting battle or disaster casualties to determine those who needed immediate help, those who could wait, and those who were beyond help.

REALITY CHECK

I thought about my family and friends a lot as I was going down. I thought about my boyfriend saying I shouldn't be flying. I pictured my pastor announcing my death in church. But I felt at peace with myself. I thought, "The Lord's going to take me and I'm O.K."

Susan White, 25 (flight attendant)

Caroline B. Cooney has written more than 50 books for young adults. Her favorite thing to write about is love, but most teenagers like her suspense and horror novels best. *Face on the Milk Carton* and, its sequel, *Whatever Happened to Janie?* were featured in a May 1995 made-for-TV movie.

Template 5.2. Flush Flash.

Template 5.3. Invitation.

"TRIAGE:
A GAME OF RESCUE AND SURVIVAL"

OBJECT OF THE GAME:

Get all three triage colors in a row across, diagonally, or down. (You must have all four squares marked in the row. You will have two of the same color.)

DIRECTIONS:

Pick a Rescue card. Follow the directions on the card. If the discussion leader at your table thinks you have fulfilled the requirements on the Rescue card, you may mark an "X" on ONE dot of the same color on this "TRIAGE" card. Once you have chosen and marked a dot, you may not change it. The first person to get the triage row wins. If time allows, keep playing until everyone has marked a row of triage colors.

Color Pattern 4

G	R	Y	Y
R	Y	R	G
Y	G	B	R
G	R	R	Y

Color Pattern 5

R	Y	G	R
Y	G	R	Y
G	R	Y	G
B	B	G	R

Color Pattern 1

B	R	Y	Y
R	Y	G	R
Y	G	R	Y
R	R	Y	G

Color Pattern 2

G	R	Y	Y
Y	Y	G	R
G	G	R	B
R	R	Y	G

Color Pattern 3

Y	G	G	R
G	B	R	Y
R	G	Y	G
Y	Y	G	R

Make five (5) different cards for each table of players using the above color patterns.

Template 5.4. "TRIAGE" Game Board and Color Pattern Chart. (Enlarge on photocopier as needed.)

From *Fiction, Food, and Fun.* © 1998. Closter, Sipes, Thomas. Libraries Unlimited. (800) 237-6124.

Template 5.5. Rescue Card Back.

1

Think!

How do you think the plane crash changed Heidi's life?

Red

2

Think!
In what ways did the crash of Flight #116 change Heidi's view of herself?

Red

3

Think!
Why do you need to put your own ego aside to be an effective EMT?

Red

4

Think!
Describe how the crash changed the relationship between Daniel and his father.

Red

5

Think!
How does the old saying "Be careful what you wish for, you just might get it", apply to Patrick?

Red

6

Think!

Why do you think Darienne was so self-centered?

Red

Template 5.6a. Rescue Card Face (questions).

From *Fiction, Food, and Fun.* © 1998. Closter, Sipes, Thomas. Libraries Unlimited. (800) 237-6124.

7

Think!
**Explain how Patrick's
family life influenced his
decision to become an
EMT.**

Red

8

Think!
**Describe how Heidi's
background was different
from Patrick's.**

Red

9

Think!
**Explain why Heidi's
parents change their
opinion of their daughter.**

Red

10

Think!
**Describe Shirl's thoughts
as she waited at the airport
for news of Flight #116.**

Red

11

Think!
**Why is this novel called
"realistic fiction"?**

Red

12

Think!
**How does Patrick change
because of his experience
with the crash of Flight
#116?**

Red

Template 5.6b. Rescue Card Face (questions).

13

Think!
Explain how Patrick's family life influenced his decision to become an EMT.

Red

14

Think!
Project an epilogue for this novel. What do you think will happen between Heidi and Patrick in the months to come?

Red

15

Think!
How are some of Heidi's and Patrick's problems very much like some that you face?

Red

16

Think!
Explain why people feel useless in a situation like that of a plane crash.

Red

1

Comprehend!
Why is the time included at the beginning of each chapter? How is this information useful?

Yellow

2

Comprehend!
Where is Carly going? Who is going to meet her at the airport?

Yellow

Template 5.6c. Rescue Card Face (questions).

3

Comprehend!

Tell three things that would complete this statement: Heidi is ___, ___, and ___.

Yellow

4

Comprehend!

What did Heidi do to try to comfort Carly?

Yellow

5

Comprehend!

What problems do the rescue workers deal with at the crash site?

Yellow

6

Comprehend!

Who was nicknamed "Honeybun"?

Yellow

7

Comprehend!

What does yellow mean in the triage?

Yellow

8

Comprehend!

What was "Life Star"?

Yellow

Template 5.6d. Rescue Card Face (questions).

9

Comprehend!

What is the "golden hour"?

Yellow

10

Comprehend!

What does green mean in the triage?

Yellow

11

Comprehend!
Why did the town of Nearing River train high school students as emergency rescue personnel?
Yellow

12

Comprehend!

Why was Teddie so upset about losing her quarter?

Yellow

13

Comprehend!

What were the first things Heidi did to help the people of Flight #116?

Yellow

14

Comprehend!

How much time elapses from the beginning of the book to the end?

Yellow

Template 5.6e. Rescue Card Face (questions).

15

Comprehend!

What does red mean in the triage?

Yellow

16

Comprehend!

What kinds of things were important to Darienne?

Yellow

1

Role-Play/Research
A baby is born on the highway in the traffic jam that results from the crash of the plane. Ask an EMT what help can be given to someone who is having a baby. Share your answer with your table.
Green

2

Role-Play/Research
Ask a Red Cross volunteer what training is required to become a Red Cross volunteer. Share your answer with your table.

Green

3

Role-Play/ Research
Ask a Red Cross Volunteer how the Red Cross helps in a disaster such as the one in the book. Share the answer with your table.

Green

4

Role-Play/ Research

Ask an EMT why he or she decided to become an EMT. Share the answer with your table.

Green

Template 5.6f. Rescue Card Face (questions).

5

Role-Play/Research

Ask an EMT how to treat Teddi's injury (compound leg fracture). Share the answer with your table.

Green

6

Role-Play/Research

Ask an EMT to describe the circumstances when he or she had to tag a victim with a triage color.

Green

7

Role-Play/Research
You are Patrick. Choose someone at your table to be your father. Argue about whether you should be allowed to continue working on the disaster site after the senior EMTs arrive.
Green

8

Role-Play/Research
You are Daniel. Your father and your future stepmother come to see you in the hospital after the disaster. What is the first thing you say to them?

Green

9

Role-Play/Research
You are Teddi's father waiting at the airport for her to arrive. An airline employee tells you Teddi's plane has crashed. What questions would be going through your head?

Green

10

Role-Play/Research
You are Darienne. Choose someone at your table to act as a TV reporter. Give an interview about your experiences during the plane crash.

Green

Template 5.6g. Rescue Card Face (questions).

11

Role-Play/Research

You are Ty. Tell the others at your table about your contributions to the rescue effort.

Green

12

Role-Play/ Research
Ask a Red Cross volunteer to describe how you could help during a local disaster. Share the answer with your table.

Green

13

Role-Play/Research

You are Mrs. Jemmison. What are some of the things you say to Daniel to keep his spirits up?

Green

14

Role-Play/Research
You are in charge of the rescue operation. Explain to your team things they need to do to take care of themselves so that they can take care of others.
Green

15

Role-Play/Research
You are a TV reporter who has been at the scene all night. Choose a person at your table to be Patrick's father. Interview him "on the air" about the rescue efforts.
Green

16

Role-Play/Research
Ask an EMT what the black color on the triage tag represents. Share his/her answer with your table.

Green

Template 5.6h. Rescue Card Face (questions).

From *Fiction, Food, and Fun.* © 1998. Closter, Sipes, Thomas. Libraries Unlimited. (800) 237-6124.

SORRY! YOU MAY NOT USE ONE ROW THAT CONTAINS A BLACK DOT!

SORRY! YOU MAY NOT USE ONE ROW THAT CONTAINS A BLACK DOT!

SORRY! YOU MAY NOT USE ONE ROW THAT CONTAINS A BLACK DOT!

SORRY! YOU MAY NOT USE ONE ROW THAT CONTAINS A BLACK DOT!

SORRY! YOU MAY NOT USE ONE ROW THAT CONTAINS A BLACK DOT!

SORRY! YOU MAY NOT USE ONE ROW THAT CONTAINS A BLACK DOT!

Template 5.7. Rescue Death Card Face.

READ 'n' FEED

Flight #116 Is Down

Agenda

_____	(10 min.) Serve and seat participants, begin eating
_____	(5 min.) Begin discussion
_____	(5 min.) Introduction of guests
_____	(20 min.) Play "TRIAGE"
_____	(5 min.) Dismissal

TRIAGE:
A Game of Rescue and Survival

Facilitators: This is a working lunch. Begin the discussion described below as soon as everyone has arrived at your table. Discussion continues until the guests are introduced to the entire group. At that point, "TRIAGE" play begins.

Read the cards provided in your packet quoting survivors of a plane crash. Ask students to compare the quotes with the dialogue of the survivors in the novel. Does the book treat the survivors realistically?

Directions: Play "TRIAGE: A Game of Rescue and Survival." "TRIAGE" is played like Bingo. The object of the game is to complete a row of four across, down, or diagonally. The first players to mark a row that includes each of the three triage colors — red, green, and yellow — wins.

Play begins with the student to the left of the facilitator. The player draws a card from the Rescue card deck and reads the question aloud. The player must answer the question or follow the directions given on the Rescue card. Note what color the card is coded: yellow, green, or red. If the discussion leader thinks the player fulfills the requirement as requested on the Rescue card, then the player marks an *X* on one of his or her game card color dots. The player must choose a dot that matches the color at the bottom of the Rescue card he or she just played. If a player draws a Rescue card with the skull and crossbones, one row on that player's game card with the black dot in it "dies" and cannot be used to win.

Play continues to the left until a player wins by marking a row containing all three triage colors: red, yellow, and green.

Template 5.8. Agenda and Activity Instructions.

From *Fiction, Food, and Fun.* © 1998. Closter, Sipes, Thomas. Libraries Unlimited. (800) 237-6124.

Chapter **6**

Maniac Magee

Bibliographic Information

Jerry Spinelli. *Maniac Magee*. New York: Harper Trophy, 1990. 184 pages. $3.95. ISBN 0-06-440424-2.

Interest Level

Grades 5 through 8

Themes

Relationships, Friendship, Racial Prejudice, Family Structure, Homelessness, Illiteracy, Survival, Baseball

Plot Summary

After his parents die, Jeffrey Lionel Magee's life becomes legendary, as he accomplishes athletic and other feats that awe his contemporaries.

Author Information

Jerry Spinelli grew up in Norristown, Pennsylvania, where every kid had a nickname, and the sandlots and woods were filled with legends like Maniac Magee. Spinelli dreamed of becoming a major league baseball player but changed his career goals after a poem he wrote about his high school football team's victory was published in the local newspaper. He worked for 22 years as an editor for a business magazine to support his family and during that time wrote four unpublished novels before *Space Station Seventh Grade* was published in 1982.

Spinelli is probably best known for *Maniac Magee*. This 1990 novel won numerous book awards, among which were the *Boston Globe*/Horn Book Award and the Newbery Medal. The people and events in *Maniac Magee* were borrowed from his childhood, his children, and from readers he met. Jeffrey Lionel Magee grew out of his experiences with prejudice as a youth. A friend, orphaned at nine months and raised in an orphanage, was refused entry to the public swimming pool in town. Until then, the friend had only known that he was black; now he knew that it made a difference. The real "Amanda" was a sixth grader from a school in New York State who brought her entire home library of books to school each day in a suitcase.

Spinelli was educated at Gettysburg College, Johns Hopkins University, and Temple University. He and his wife, who is also a writer, have seven children. Spinelli is popular with young adult readers because he writes about adolescent problems with humor, honesty, realism, and believable dialogue. Other books by Spinelli are *Jason and Marceline, Who Put That Hair in My Toothbrush?* and *There's a Girl in My Hammerlock.*

Booktalk

They say Maniac Magee was born in a dump. They say his stomach was a cereal box and his heart a sofa spring. They say he kept an eight-inch cockroach on a leash and that rats stood guard over him while he slept. They say if you knew he was coming and you sprinkled salt on the ground and he ran over it, within two or three blocks he would be as slow as everybody else. They say.

Now Maniac wasn't his real name, but they say that's what just about everyone called him because he dared to do things no other kids would do. They say he lived with a family in the East End of Two Mills when only Black families lived there. And that he rescued John Arnold from Mr. Finsterwald's backyard when no White kid from the West End would even deliver papers to the house. They say he hit John McNab's famous fastball and bunted the world's first frogball for a four-bagger. They say he took a bite off Mars Bar Thompson's candy bar and successfully untied the famous Cobble's Knot. He could catch the longest passes and kick the longest punts . . . they say. Maniac was always running and, as incredible as it may seem, they say he could even run down the railroad tracks on the rail!

They say Maniac was an orphan ever since a train accident killed both of his parents. They say, in a sense, he was also blind. They say he couldn't see why the kids on the East End of town didn't like him or what the big deal was about whether a person was Black or White. Most of all, they say he was blind to the fact that some kids don't like you when you're not like them. He couldn't see why they didn't like you if you didn't watch cartoons on Saturday morning, or did dishes without being told, or were allergic to pizza, or showed them up and made them look bad—especially if you were a different color.

Sure, the folks in Two Mills remember Maniac. Do they remember what's true or what's myth? Well, it's hard to know. Most all of them will say they remember what Maniac did for the kids on the East End and the kids on the West End.

Sign up today to come to the *Maniac Magee* READ 'n' FEED. Don't miss this legend.

What's Cookin' at the READ 'n' FEED?

The story of Jeffrey "Maniac" Magee is a modern-day tall tale. Jeffrey is an orphan who longs to have a place to call home and who creatively finds solutions to the conflicts he encounters in the racially segregated town of Two Mills, Pennsylvania. In focusing on the problems of homeless people, students move from Tall Tales to Conflicts to Hopes and Fears to Solutions and finally, to Legacy. As they relocate from one discussion station to the next, they respond to questions and try to "untangle" the conflicts and myths in Jeffrey's life. The culminating activity for each group is to write and perform a jump rope chant about Maniac Magee. The setting depicts Cobble's Corner pizza place, complete with the famed Cobble's Knot, red-and-white tablecloths, and a menu of pizza and butterscotch Krimpets.

Preparations

Read "The Recipe for a Successful READ 'n' FEED Program" at the beginning of this book for a discussion of those materials, designs, resources, and handouts needed for every READ 'n' FEED. Be sure to copy the Planning Outline and Program Checklist form in the appendix of this book, so you will have it ready for your first design team meeting. In addition, the *Maniac Magee* program requires discussion station signs, a set of brainstorming charts, and facilitator question guides for each discussion table.

SHOPPING LIST

- Purple crayons or markers
- Recordings of polka music
- Jump ropes
- Table coverings, plates, napkins, cups, dinnerware as needed
- Materials for decorations as described in the "Whipping Up the Fun" section of this chapter
- Duplicating paper: white and tan
- Construction paper: white, cream, tan, and various shades of brown

ADDING THE GARNISHES

- Bunting, Eve. *Fly Away Home.* New York: Clarion Books, 1991.
- Burton, Virginia Lee. *Mike Mulligan and His Steam Shovel.* Boston: Houghton Mifflin, 1939.
- de Brunhoff, Jean. *The Story of Babar, the Little Elephant.* New York: Random House, 1960.
- Piper, Watty. *The Little Engine That Could.* New York: Platt and Munk, 1961, c1930.
- Polette, Nancy. *Novel Booktalks: Award Winners and Other Favorites.* Vol. 2. O'Fallon, MO: Book Lures, 1992.
- Waber, Bernard. *Lyle, Lyle, Crocodile.* Boston: Houghton Mifflin, 1965.

Also check your school or public library for video documentaries on the plight of homeless children and adults or for animated films of American tall tales, like Pecos Bill, Paul Bunyan, Casey Jones, Mike Fink, or John Henry.

FOOD FOR THOUGHT

Plan a menu that includes pizza and butterscotch Krimpets; sponge cake with butterscotch icing will substitute for Krimpets. Consider other foods mentioned in the novel such as spaghetti, chocolate cake with white icing, carrots, apples, grilled chicken or ribs, zeps (a type of hoagie), steak sandwiches, strombolis, meatloaf, mashed potatoes and gravy, zucchini, salad, and coconut custard pie. Place bite-sized candy (Mars Bar Thompson's signature brand!) at each place setting.

WHIPPING UP THE FUN

Publicize the program. Copy the publicity poster (Template 6.1) and the Flush Flash (Template 6.2). Add local event details before displaying these promotional templates. Write a student announcement using the sample in the "Booktalk" section of this chapter. Distribute the book to the students along with a schedule of event dates and expectation deadlines. (See the sample Student Time Line Memo in the appendix at the end of this book.)

Following the student sign-up period, decide the number of students you will seat at each discussion table and the number of tables and discussion facilitators you will need. Remember that there are five discussion stations; however, students will only rotate among four of them. Therefore, the number of tables you will need must be a multiple of four.

Select facilitators and designate which discussion station they will facilitate: Tall Tales, Conflicts, Hopes and Fears, or Solutions. All facilitators will help with Legacy, the fifth discussion station. Along with a copy of the novel to read, include copies of the Legacy Facilitator's Guide (Template 6.21), the specific facilitator's guide (either Template 6.17, 6.18, 6.19, or 6.20) and Discussion Charts (Templates 6.10–6.16) for the station assigned to them. The related discussion charts are noted on each facilitator's guide. A week before the READ 'n' FEED program, supply facilitators with any special instructions about the activities (outlined in Template 6.22).

Copy several pages from the "A" volume of an encyclopedia. Shred pages for confetti to be used in decorations.

The street signs (Template 6.4) can help you create table identification signs and seating tags. Enlarge the individual street signs on Template 6.4 to 8.5-x-14 inches. Copy each sign on a shade of brown construction paper. Lay the sign on the table or attach the street sign to a two- to three-foot-long piece of cardboard tubing and stand the sign in the middle of the table. Prepare seating tags by copying Template 6.4 on the same shade of brown paper. Trim and sort street names, keeping only those names you are using for table identification. The number of students attending and the number of tables will determine how many street signs and seating tags you need.

Templates 6.5 through 6.9 are signs to label the five discussion stations. Copy the Legacy sign (Template 6.9) for each table. Make one copy of the Tall Tales sign (Template 6.5), Conflicts sign (Template 6.6), Hopes and Fears sign (Template 6.7), and Solutions sign (Template 6.8) for every four tables you have in your seating arrangement. Mount the signs on brown construction paper. If you have more than four tables, mount the second set of signs on a different shade of brown.

Copy the *Maniac Magee* Discussion Charts (Templates 6.10–6.16) so that each table has a complete set of charts. Staple each set to an easel. A description for a simple, easy-to-make easel is included in the "Hints for a Gourmet READ 'n' FEED" section of this chapter.

Plan and prepare decorations to represent one of the settings from the novel. Create the Cobble's Corner storefront with bulletin board paper and lots of creative ingenuity! You can even have a Cobble's Knot hanging from the American flag stand. Cover the tables with red-and-white plastic tablecloths with cardboard poles placed in the center to display the street signs and discussion station signs. "Outside" the storefront, scatter the confetti from the Volume A encyclopedia.

Red, white, and blue bunting, flags, and picnic paraphernalia can transform a room into a Fourth of July block party for an alternative to the Cobble's Corner theme. A third possibility is to create the baseball-equipment room at the back of the park band shell. Use chest protectors, equipment bags, balls, bats, and mitts, adding decorations like Grayson and Maniac had for Christmas.

Copy the invitation (Template 6.3) on tan paper to use as admission into the READ 'n' FEED program. Address this invitation to students who qualify to attend the program.

Plan an agenda, allowing at least 60 minutes to complete the activities. Allot 10 minutes at each discussion station before signaling students to move to the next station. Allow some time at the end of the program for each group to perform its jump rope chant.

Assemble the facilitators' packets. In each packet, include a place card with the facilitator's name, a copy of the novel, the Agenda and Activity Instructions, a copy of the discussion questions for the particular station assigned to that facilitator, and a thank-you note. Place the packet on the appropriate table.

Confirm this list of materials for each table: street/table identification sign; two discussion station signs (Legacy and one other); facilitator's packet; easel displaying the seven discussion charts; purple marker or crayon; Mars Bar Thompson's favorite candy at each setting; a jump rope; and any other theme decorations.

Whetting Their Appetite

Select one of these program ideas to prepare your students for the *Maniac Magee* READ 'n' FEED program:

- Read aloud the story *Fly Away Home*. Show a short segment from a film or news documentary on the homeless. Discuss this problem in your community. What conflicts or problems do people, particularly children, experience when they do not have a home?

- Arrange students in small "story hour" circles on the floor. Within each circle, read aloud one of the children's picture books mentioned in the novel and follow up with a group exchange of memorable childhood reading experiences.

- Show a short segment from an animated tall tale such as Pecos Bill. Discuss the larger than life feats of the hero. Explain that *Maniac Magee* is also a tall tale and that students will be examining and comparing Maniac's feats with those of other tall tale heroes during the READ 'n' FEED program.

- Organize a Raggedy, Flap-Soled, Smelly Tennis Shoe Contest or a Cobble's Knot Challenge. Participants cast ballots for the grubbiest shoe or try to untie the grungy "Cobble's Knot." Ask local pizza restaurants to donate coupons for free pizza to the winners.

Mixing the Fiction, Food, and Fun

Polka music is playing as students enter. Students receive seating tags as they check in. After picking up their food, they locate the table with the street sign that matches the color and name of their tag.

Students begin at either the Tall Tales, Conflicts, Hopes and Fears, or Solutions station. They remain at each station for 10 minutes before moving as a group to the next station. Each group takes its discussion easel to the next station. The rotation order follows: Tall Tales to Conflicts to Hopes and Fears to Solutions and back to Tall Tales, depending on where the group started the rotation. At the end of the fourth discussion, all stations change to Legacy and proceed with the activity planned for that discussion. Facilitators remain at their original discussion station throughout the program.

Facilitators guide students through the discussion of *Maniac Magee* as they ask questions related to their station, help students brainstorm and chart their thoughts, and encourage them in creating a jump rope chant.

Hints for a Gourmet READ 'n' FEED

Set up a simple database report to make it easier for you to verify student participation and attendance, student homerooms, book circulation, and student testing results.

If you have more than four tables, consider using color coding or a number identification with the street signs and discussion station signs. For example, the first group of four discussion stations could feature white street signs, station signs, and tags while the next group of four stations could feature light brown signs and tags. Students then rotate through stations within the same color code.

Serve the students' meals on cafeteria trays as they will be moving from station to station.

Consider the discussion abilities of the students participating; certain discussion questions can be omitted or reworded to accommodate the capabilities of the students.

Carry out the color theme where possible. Read Maniac Magee's description of the people colors of the East End (on page 51 of the paperback edition of the novel) and then his analysis of his own color (on page 58 of the paperback edition of the novel).

Discussion easels are helpful and can be purchased from art supply stores or easily made from corrugated cardboard or art foam core. Cut 9-x-12-inch rectangles from the cardboard or foam core. Attach a wedge-shaped piece of cardboard or foam core to the back of each 9-x-12-inch rectangle with book repair tape so that the shorter edge of the wedge is centered and the wider edge is flush with the bottom edge of the rectangle. The wedge should be six to seven inches in height and measure about two inches across the top edge and about four inches across the bottom edge. The wedge forms a "leg," like the support on the back of a picture frame. Attach a three-inch length of yarn or wide elastic to the lower part of the wedge across to that same position on the rectangle so the easel will be freestanding. Discussion charts or blank drawing paper can now be stapled to the top front of the easel. Figure 6.1 illustrates how to cut and assemble the easel.

The preliminary program should include a description of how students will be seated and an explanation of the discussion activity. Emphasize that students will move from station to station during the READ 'n' FEED program.

Find a facilitator who is a good whistler. Use the "Pickwell whistle" as the signal to eat, change discussion stations, or make any other transition.

Don't forget to evaluate your program. Student and facilitator comments will help you revise future READ 'n' FEED programs. A sample evaluation form is included in the appendix at the end of this book.

Easel

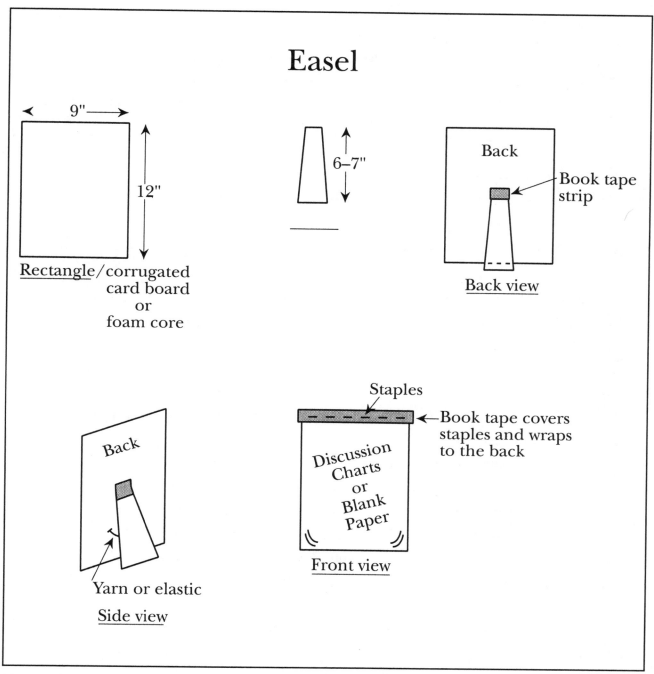

Figure 6.1.

Novel Connections

- Organize a food or clothing drive for a homeless shelter in your community.
- Edit and refine jump rope chants to create poems and rap songs that reflect on the themes, humor, or wisdom of *Maniac Magee.* Create an exhibit using these students' writings to display within your school or the local public library. Submit some of the poems to be published in your school's literary magazine.

- Encourage students to write their version of "The Man Who Struck Out Willie Mays" to display at a Young Authors Conference.

- Research minor league baseball and the Toledo Mud Hens. Find someone in the community who might have played minor league ball during the 1950s to speak to students.

- Call the local literacy coalition to see how students can help. Design a literacy project for your school in which older students read aloud to younger children.

More Book Bites

Avi. *Blue Heron*. New York: Avon Camelot, 1993.

Cole, Brock. *The Goats*. New York: Farrar, Straus & Giroux, 1992.

Deuker, Carl. *Heart of a Champion*. New York: Avon Flare, 1994.

Fox, Paula. *Monkey Island*. New York: Dell, 1993.

George, Jean Craighead. *My Side of the Mountain*. New York: Puffin Books, 1991.

Gutman, Dan. *Baseball's Greatest Games*. New York: Puffin Books, 1996.

Guy, Rosa. *The Friends*. New York: Dell, 1996.

Hahn, Mary Downing. *December Stillness*. New York: Avon Flare, 1990.

Holman, Felice. *Slake's Limbo*. New York: Aladdin Books, 1986.

Klein, Robin. *Came Back to Show You I Could Fly*. New York: Viking Penguin, 1989.

Lowry, Lois. *Rabble Starkey*. Boston: Houghton Mifflin, 1987.

Myers, Walter Dean. *Darnell Rock Reporting*. New York: Delacorte Press, 1994.

Nelson, Theresa. *The Beggar's Ride*. New York: Dell, 1994.

Neufeld, John. *Almost a Hero*. New York: Atheneum, 1995.

Osborne, Mary Pope. *American Tall Tales*. New York: Alfred A. Knopf, 1991.

Paterson, Katherine. *The Great Gilly Hopkins*. New York: Harper Trophy, 1987.

Paulsen, Gary. *The Monument*. New York: Dell, 1993.

Sachs, Marilyn. *At the Sound of the Beep*. New York: Dutton Childrens, 1990.

Sleator, William. *Oddballs: Stories*. New York: Puffin Books, 1995.

Taylor, Mildred. *Roll of Thunder, Hear My Cry*. New York: Puffin Books, 1991.

Taylor, Theodore. *The Cay*. New York: Avon Camelot, 1977.

Voigt, Cynthia. *Dicey's Song*. New York: Fawcett Junier, 1987.

Walker, Paul Robert. *Big Men, Big Country: A Collection of American Tall Tales*. San Diego: Harcourt Brace, 1993.

Templates

Publicity Poster, Template 6.1

Flush Flash, Template 6.2

Student Invitation, Template 6.3

Street Signs, Template 6.4

Tall Tales Station Sign, Template 6.5

Conflicts Station Sign, Template 6.6

Hopes and Fears Station Sign, Template 6.7

Solutions Station Sign, Template 6.8

Legacy Station Sign, Template 6.9

Discussion Chart (*Maniac Magee* 1), Template 6.10

Discussion Chart (*Maniac Magee* 2), Template 6.11

Discussion Chart (*Maniac Magee* 3), Template 6.12

Discussion Chart (*Maniac Magee* 4), Template 6.13

Discussion Chart (*Maniac Magee* 5), Template 6.14

Discussion Chart (*Maniac Magee* 6), Template 6.15

Discussion Chart (*Maniac Magee* 7), Template 6.16

Tall Tales Facilitator's Guide, Template 6.17

Conflicts Facilitator's Guide, Template 6.18

Hopes and Fears Facilitator's Guide, Template 6.19

Solutions Facilitator's Guide, Template 6.20

Legacy Facilitator's Guide, Template 6.21

Agenda and Activity Instructions, Template 6.22

READ 'n' FEED

READ 'n' FEED
Maniac Magee
by Jerry Spinelli

Fiction: *Maniac Magee* by Jerry Spinelli

_____
(Date)

Food:

Fun: You'll tell a tall tale or two,
untangle a few knots in Maniac's life,
and get an aerobic workout!

Be sure to reserve your copy of this
month's featured novel.

Sign up _____
(Date)

in _____◆
(Room)

Listen to announcements for further details.

Template 6.1. Publicity Poster.

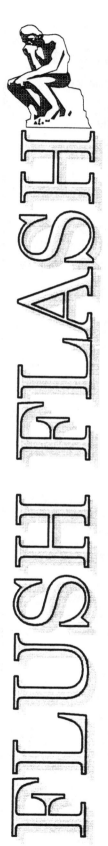

FLUSH FLASH

Maniac Magee

by Jerry Spinelli

Jeffrey "Maniac" Magee is a legend in Two Mills, Pennsylvania. Read this month's featured novel to learn about his headline news:

Maniac amazes local viewers

This week, West End kids witnessed Maniac Magee hit a telephone pole with a stone 61 times in a row. Residents of Rako Hill saw him walk through the nearby rat-infested dump barefoot! Local fishermen say he . . .

Unusual allergy causes outbreak

Doctors are puzzled by pepperoni-sized blotches covering local boy's body. Pizza is thought to have caused the rash, however . . .

Date:

READ 'N' FEED

Courageous teen saves boy from Finsterwallies

After hearing screams from the backyard at 803 Oriole, neighbors watched Maniac Magee carry the limp carcass of John Arnold to safety. They . . .

Runaway found with buffalo at zoo

Police are searching for the parents of a runaway who has been living in the buffalo pen at the Elmwood Park Zoo for . . .

Sponsored by

Template 6.2. Flush Flash.

From *Fiction, Food, and Fun.* © 1998. Closter, Sipes, Thomas. Libraries Unlimited. (800) 237-6124.

You've tried the rest
Now try the best!

DINE IN
OR
CARRY OUT

ALL YOU CAN EAT
PIZZA BUFFET
EVERY TUESDAY
$4.99
Also specializing in
strombolis, steak sandwiches, and
zeps,
Two Mills famous hoagies!

Reservations
646-5772

COBBLE'S CORNER
Corner of Hector and Birch

Hurry! Limited time offer!

See Maniac Magee untie the famous Cobble's Knot! This could be your last chance.

Free Admission

PRESENT THIS
COUPON TO ENTER
THE READ 'N' FEED
Name_____
_____
Room_____

You've tried the rest
Now try the best!

DINE IN
OR
CARRY OUT

ALL YOU CAN EAT
PIZZA BUFFET
EVERY TUESDAY
$4.99
Also specializing in
strombolis, steak sandwiches, and
zeps,
Two Mills famous hoagies!

Reservations
646-5772

COBBLE'S CORNER
Corner of Hector and Birch

Hurry! Limited time offer!

See Maniac Magee untie the famous Cobble's Knot! This could be your last chance.

Free Admission

PRESENT THIS
COUPON TO ENTER
THE READ 'N' FEED
Name_____
_____
Room_____

Template 6.3. Student Invitation.

803 W. Oriole

N. Hector

709 E. Chestnut

W. Green

E. Arch

E. Marshall

W. Moore

W. Elm

728 E. Sycamore

E. Birch

101 Band Shell Blvd

Template 6.4. Street Signs. (Enlarge on photocopier as needed.)

Maniac Magee

TALL TALES

"The history of a kid is one part fact, two parts legend and three parts snowball."

Template 6.5. Tall Tales Station Sign.

Maniac Magee

CONFLICTS

"*Maniac loved almost eveything about his new life. But everything did not love him back.*"

Template 6.6. Conflicts Station Sign.

Maniac Magee

HOPES and FEARS

Run, run, as fast as you can. You can't catch me, I'm the Maniac Man!

Template 6.7. Hopes and Fears Station Sign.

Maniac Magee

SOLUTIONS

"How could he act as a father to these boys, when he himself ached to be somebody's son?"

Template 6.8. Solutions Station Sign.

Maniac Magee

LEGACY

Ma-niac, Ma-niac
He's so *cool*
Ma-niac, Ma-niac
Don't go to *school*
Runs all *night*
Runs all *right*
Ma-niac, Ma-niac
Kissed a *bull!*

Template 6.9. Legacy Station Sign.

What makes a legend?

Tall Tale Heroes	Maniac Magee

Maniac Magee 1

Template 6.10. Discussion Chart (*Maniac Magee* 1).

Maniac's Amazing Feats

Myth:_____

Truth:_____

Myth:_____

Truth:_____

Myth:_____

Truth:_____

Myth:_____

Truth:_____

Myth:_____

Truth:_____

Myth:_____

Truth:_____

Myth:_____

Truth:_____

Myth:_____

Truth:_____

Maniac Magee 2

Template 6.11. Discussion Chart (*Maniac Magee* 2).

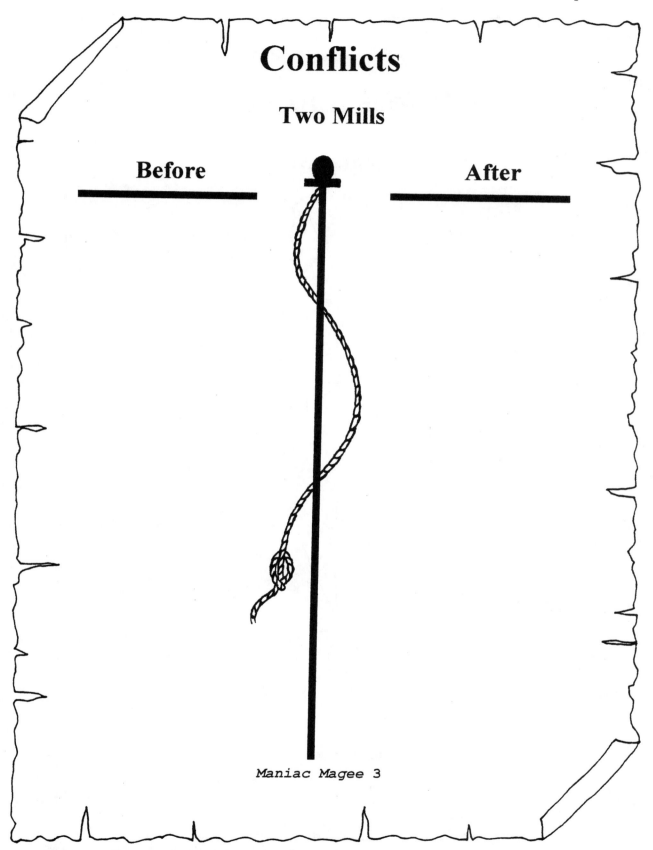

Conflicts

Two Mills

Before   **After**

Maniac Magee 3

Template 6.12. Discussion Chart (*Maniac Magee* 3).

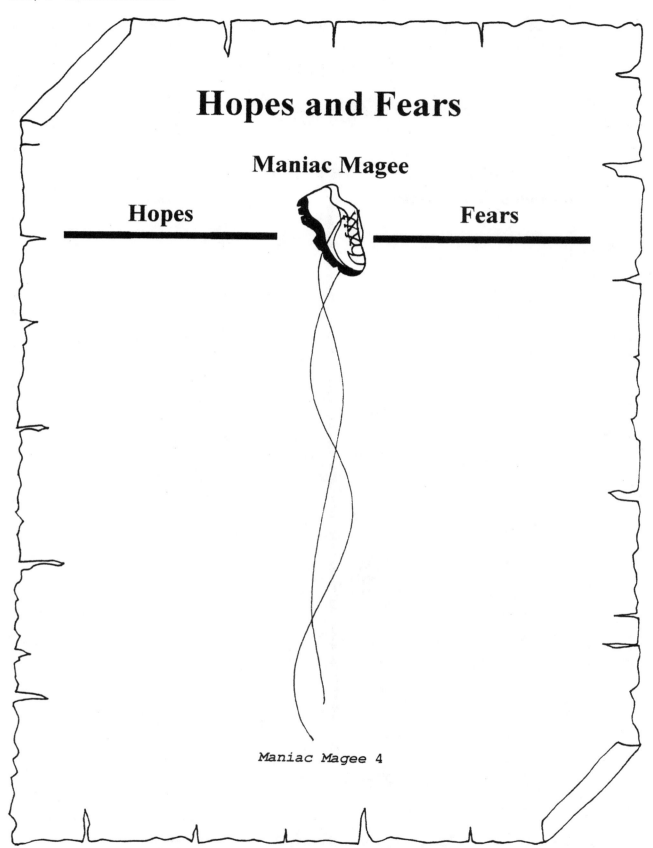

Hopes and Fears

Maniac Magee

Hopes   **Fears**

Maniac Magee 4

Template 6.13. Discussion Chart (*Maniac Magee* 4).

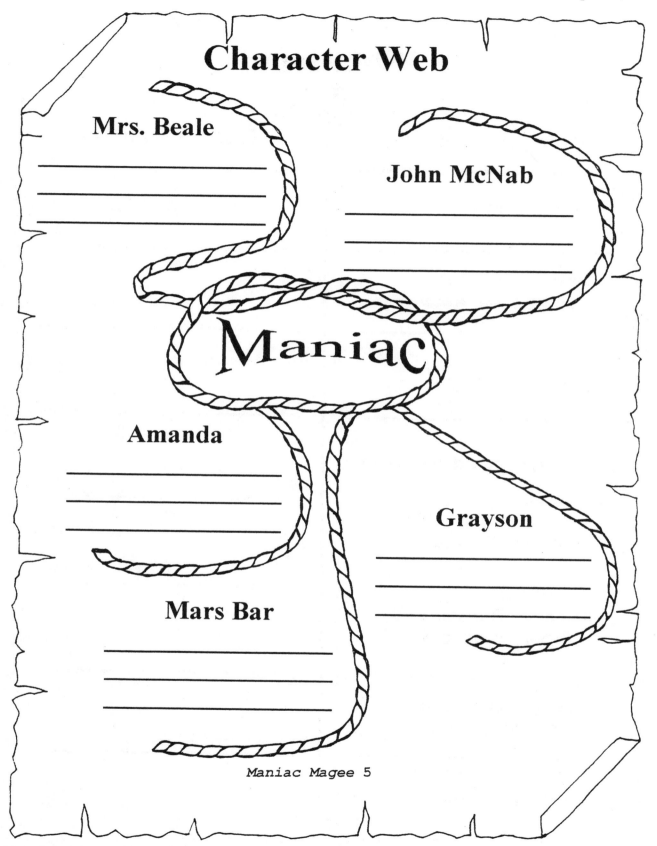

Character Web

Mrs. Beale

John McNab

Maniac

Amanda

Grayson

Mars Bar

Maniac Magee 5

Template 6.14. Discussion Chart (*Maniac Magee* 5).

Solutions

Situation/Challenge	Maniac's Solution
Cobble's Knot	
Lester and Hester writing on walls	
Graffiti on Beale's house	
Grayson could not read	
Death of Grayson	
Keeping Russell and Piper in school	
The McNabs dare to go into East End	
Russell stranded on trolley trestle	

Maniac Magee 6

Template 6.15. Discussion Chart (*Maniac Magee* 6).

LEGACY
Jump Rope Chant

Maniac Magee 7

Template 6.16. Discussion Chart (*Maniac Magee 7*).

Volume 101	**Two Mills Times**	**Tall Tales**
Two Mills, PA		Facilitator's Guide

The story of Maniac Magee is a modern-day tall tale, including plenty of great and daring feats that make Maniac a legendary kid. This extraordinary athlete overcomes seemingly impossible obstacles and touches the lives of many people with his kindness and wisdom.

1. Discuss heroes from other American tall tales that you know. What qualities make them legends? Record your answer on the left-hand side of *Maniac Magee* 1!

2. How does Jeffrey Lionel Magee get his nickname? Do you think "Maniac" is a good name for him? What other names might you have given him?

3. How is Maniac similar to the heroes in the other tall tales you have read? Record your comparison on the right-hand side of *Maniac Magee* 1!

4. Maniac performs many amazing feats. Describe as many of the larger-than-life exaggerations that make Maniac a legend. Record your list on the "Myth" sections of *Maniac Magee* 2!

5. Do these exaggerations capture your interest and make you want to read more? Explain.

6. Look at your list of Maniac's amazing feats. Rewrite the myths to describe what you think is more than likely what he really did. Record these on the "Truth" sections of *Maniac Magee* 2!

7. Why do you think the author decides to make Maniac a "legend" instead of an ordinary boy?

8. Discuss the way in which Maniac's story is written. How is *Maniac Magee* different from other books you have read? Did you like this style? Why or why not?

Template 6.17. Tall Tales Facilitator's Guide.

Volume 102

Two Mills, PA

Two Mills Times

Conflicts

Facilitator's Guide

A conflict is a situation in which a character in a story faces a problem or a struggle. The conflict may be with other people, with nature, or within the character. Maniac faces predicaments that take his life on many unexpected turns.

1. What early conflicts in Maniac's life cause him to arrive in Two Mills as a ragged, homeless boy? Record your examples on the "Before" side of *Maniac Magee* 3!

2. Discuss the conflicts that Maniac faces once he gets to Two Mills. Record your examples on the "After" side of *Maniac Magee* 3!

3. Racial segregation is the conflict that divides the town of Two Mills.
   a. What are Maniac's feeling toward White people? Toward Black people?
   b. Discuss the meaning of the phrase "color blind." How is Maniac color blind?
   c. How does racial segregation cause conflicts for Maniac Magee?
   d. Describe what Mars Bar Thompson does after Maniac takes a bite of his candy. Why does Mars Bar react this way?

4. How does the community's attitude toward racial segregation affect these characters: Amanda, John McNab, Hester and Lester, Russell and Piper, Mars Bar, Grayson, Mrs. Beale?

5. Why do you think Maniac suddenly hugs and squeezes Mrs. Beale after she slaps him for bringing "the vacant lot into her kitchen"?

6. Why is Maniac unable to live with the McNabs any longer?

Template 6.18. Conflicts Facilitator's Guide.

From *Fiction, Food, and Fun.* © 1998. Closter, Sipes, Thomas. Libraries Unlimited. (800) 237-6124.

Two Mills Times

Volume 103

Two Mills, PA

Hopes and Fears
Facilitator's Guide

Maniac just keeps running, wishing he could settle in, but always fearing that something will happen to the people he cares for.

1. After Maniac meets Grayson, we learn more about Maniac's thoughts and feelings. Describe what you think are his hopes and fears for the future. Be sure to record these on *Maniac Magee* 4!

2. What causes the fear that divides the East Side and West Side of Two Mills from each other?

3. What hopes and fears do you have about your future? How do they differ from those of the characters in the book?

4. Briefly discuss the characters on the Character Web chart (5). Think of at least three words that each character would use to describe Maniac from his or her point of view. Be sure to record these on *Maniac Magee* 5!

5. Why doesn't Maniac want to go to school? Does he value learning? Give examples to support your answer.

6. How does Maniac give Grayson hope?

7. How is Maniac's life with Grayson different from his life with the Beales?

8. Why does Maniac run everywhere in the novel?

9. Why do you think Maniac ran away from Grayson's funeral?

10. Do you think a young person could really survive all alone in the world the way Maniac did? Why or why not?

Template 6.19. Hopes and Fears Facilitator's Guide.

From *Fiction, Food, and Fun*. © 1998. Closter, Sipes, Thomas. Libraries Unlimited. (800) 237-6124.

Two Mills Times

Volume 104

Two Mills, PA

Solutions

Facilitator's Guide

A solution is an answer to a problem. Throughout the novel, Maniac Magee struggles to find solutions to real societal pressures that many adolescents face.

1. Discuss the situations on the Solutions chart (*Maniac Magee* 6) and the way in which Maniac resolves each challenge. Be sure to record your answers on *Maniac Magee* 6!

2. Describe how Maniac Magee feels about Grayson. Why is Maniac so proud to paint the number *101* on the door of the baseball equipment room?

3. What conflicts do the Beales encounter while Maniac is living with them? How does Maniac solve the problem?

4. What attitudes in our society are represented by these families: the Beales, the McNabs, and the Pickwells?

5. Why does Maniac bring Mars Bar to the McNab house? Does Maniac's solution work? Why or why not?

6. What eventually happens to the relationship between Maniac and Mars Bar?

7. What is a theme or message from *Maniac Magee* that author Jerry Spinelli is trying to share with his readers? How do you think Maniac would address it in our society?

8. What does Maniac want more than anything else in life? How does the Beale family help Maniac get this?

9. What do you think will happen to Maniac Magee after he moves back into the Beale home at the end of the novel?

10. How has *Maniac Magee* changed your point of view about any of the conflicts in the novel? Examples: plight of homeless children, racial prejudice, runaways, living up to reputations, adult illiteracy.

Template 6.20. Solutions Facilitator's Guide.

Two Mills Times

Volume 105
Two Mills, PA

Legacy
Facilitator's Guide

A legacy is something resulting from and left behind by an action, event, or person. As Maniac resolves the conflicts in his life, he gradually changes the community of Two Mills forever through his example.

1. What do you think is Maniac's legacy to Two Mills?

2. Write a jump rope chant about Maniac Magee and perform it. Record your chant on *Maniac Magee* 7!

Template 6.21. Legacy Facilitator's Guide.

READ 'n' FEED
Maniac Magee

Agenda

_____	(5-10 min.)	Serve and seat participants; begin eating
_____	(10 min.)	Give instructions and begin first discussion station
_____	(10 min.)	Students move to next station and begin activity
_____	(10 min.)	Students move to next station and begin activity
_____	(10 min.)	Students move to next station and begin activity
_____	(5-10 min.)	Begin Legacy discussion station
_____	(5-10 min.)	Jump rope performance station

Activity Instructions

Collect seating tags. Students should be seated at the table that matches the color and street name of their tag.

Explain to your group that they will be trying to untangle the conflicts and myths in Jeffrey "Maniac" Magee's life as they respond to questions at five different discussion stations: **Tall Tales**, **Conflicts**, **Hopes and Fears**, **Solutions**, and **Legacy.** The discussion begins at your station. Guide students through the discussion of *Maniac Magee* using questions from your facilitator's guide for this station. Encourage all students in your group to share their thoughts and ideas. Be sure to select a student to record the group's responses on the discussion charts provided. The facilitator's guide tells you which charts to use.

When you hear the "Pickwell whistle," instruct your group to move to the next discussion station. Make sure they rotate in this order: Tall Tales to Conflicts to Hopes and Fears to Solutions to Tall Tales. *If there are eight or more discussion tables, direct students to rotate within the discussion station signs matching the color or number code of your station sign.* Remind your group to take their discussion charts and easel with them each time they move.

Although you will get a new group of students each time the Pickwell whistle sounds, you remain at this discussion station. With each new group, select a new recorder and begin the same discussion.

After the third move (or the fourth discussion for each group) all discussion stations become **Legacy.** Follow the Facilitator's Guide for Legacy, encouraging your group to create a jump rope chant.

Your discussion group's last activity is to perform its jump rope chant! At the last "Pickwell whistle," the group is given a turn to "jump rope" to its chant.

Template 6.22. Agenda and Activity Instructions.

From *Fiction, Food, and Fun.* © 1998. Closter, Sipes, Thomas. Libraries Unlimited. (800) 237-6124.

Chapter 7

Missing May

Bibliographic Information

Cynthia Rylant. *Missing May*. New York: Dell, 1992. 89 pages. $3.99. ISBN 0-440-408652.

Interest Level

Grades 6 through 8

Themes

Death, Grief, Friendship

Plot Summary

After the death of the beloved aunt who raised her, 12-year-old Summer and her Uncle Ob leave their West Virginia trailer in search of the strength to go on living.

Author Information

This award-winning author has written picture books, short stories, poetry, and novels for children and young adults. Her success has grown from her ability to write with great sensitivity about the concerns of her characters. Cynthia Rylant grew up in West Virginia, living with her grandparents for a few years while her mother pursued a college degree. Much of what she experienced as a child in the small mountain towns of West Virginia has found its way into her stories. It wasn't until she was in college that she became aware of "great writing." After acquiring a master's degree in English, she began working in a children's department of a public library. It was during this time that she discovered her talent for writing the clear, evocative text that has earned her so many awards and so many loyal fans. Students will enjoy her delightful autobiography, *But I'll Be Back Again: An Album*, in which she describes her feelings about her absent father, her first kiss, falling in love, and her heroes.

Booktalk

Have you ever felt like you had to take care of someone older than you? Then you know how Summer felt. Unsure of herself, scared at times, and almost always overwhelmed. Summer and her Uncle Ob are trying to put their lives back together since the death of May, Ob's wife of many years and Summer's beloved aunt. But they are both having a hard time of it, especially Ob. Summer is worried about him; he doesn't seem to want to go on living, and if he leaves, Summer will be completely alone—a very scary thought. Then something happens that changes everything. On the same day that Ob can no longer find a reason to get out of bed, Cletus Underwood shows up at their door, and they finally figure out what they need to get past *Missing May* so much.

What's Cookin' at the READ 'n' FEED?

Newbery Award-winning *Missing May* is an excellent book to stimulate discussion of friendship, families, and loss. The setting and tone of this story are good elements to use to shape the READ 'n' FEED activities. Begin the program with the students at each table "telling the story" of a magazine photograph as the characters did in the novel. The students also exchange ideas about the character May, talking about how she might have looked and her qualities as revealed in the novel. The book discussion takes place while playing a bingo-type game. Participants each receive a bingo card with a significant word from the novel in each space. As students answer questions about the story, these words emerge as part of the discussion. Students place a token on each word as it is heard. After the discussion game, small groups of students work together to create a collage of their impression of the novel. After the *Missing May* program, all of the collages are gathered together to create a patchwork quilt to display.

Preparations

Check "The Recipe for a Successful READ 'n' FEED" at the beginning of this book for a discussion of those materials, design, resources, and handouts needed for every READ 'n' FEED program. Be sure to copy the Planning Outline and Program Checklist in the appendix of this book so you will have it ready for your first design team meeting. In addition, this program requires photographs clipped from magazines, game cards, game tokens, and art supplies for a collage.

SHOPPING LIST

- Photographs clipped from old magazines
- Whirligigs
- Pictures of the West Virginia capitol building
- Maps of West Virginia
- Battered suitcases or valises
- Table coverings, plates, napkins, cups, dinnerware as needed
- Small pieces of paper or plastic to use as game tokens
- Glue sticks
- Construction paper or bulletin board paper

ADDING THE GARNISHES

- Folktales from the Appalachian region
- Latrobe, Kathy Howard, and Mildred Knight Laughlin. *Readers Theatre for Young Adults: Scripts and Script Development.* Englewood, CO: Teacher Ideas Press, 1989.
- Rylant, Cynthia. *The Blue Hill Meadows.* San Diego: Harcourt Brace, 1997.
- ———. *But I'll Be Back Again: An Album.* New York: Orchard, 1989.
- ———. *A Couple of Kooks and Other Stories About Love.* New York: Orchard, 1990.
- ———. *A Fine White Dust.* New York: Bradbury Press, 1986.
- ———. *I Had Seen Castles.* San Diego: Harcourt Brace, 1993.
- ———. *A Kindness.* New York: Orchard, 1988.
- ———. *The Relatives Came.* New York: Bradbury Press, 1985.
- ———. *Soda Jerk.* New York: Orchard, 1990.
- ———. *This Year's Garden.* New York: Bradbury Press, 1984.
- ———. *When I Was Young in the Mountains.* New York: E. P. Dutton, 1982.
- Spiritualist information
- West Virginia Division of Tourism, 2101 Washington Street, East, Charleston, WV 25305, (800) 225-5982 or (304) 558-2286.

FOOD FOR THOUGHT

Plan a menu using some of the foods mentioned in *Missing May*: chocolate milk, turkey TV dinners, soft drinks, cookies, potato chips, candy, cocoa, watermelon, coffee, doughnuts, bacon and eggs, canned spaghetti, cereal, and honey.

WHIPPING UP THE FUN

Publicize the program at least a month in advance. Copy the Publicity Poster (Template 7.1) and the Flush Flash (Template 7.2). Add your own local event details before displaying these templates. Write a promotional announcement for your school's daily announcements, calendar of events, or newspaper, using the text from the "Booktalk" or "Plot Summary" sections of this chapter. Distribute the book to the students along with information about the date of the program and any participation requirements. (See the sample Student Time Line Memo in the appendix at the end of this book.)

Select facilitators and give each one a copy of the novel to read. At least a week before the program, supply the facilitators with any special instructions, the Agenda and Activity Instructions (Template 7.4), and the discussion questions (Templates 7.8–7.9).

Gather together old magazines containing an assortment of color photographs. Select photographs that suggest a story; you will need one photograph for each student attending the program. These photographs will be given to students as they arrive, and the students will relate their interpretation of them during introductions at each table.

Clip out approximately 25 to 35 pictures of older women, preferably individual shots rather than groups of women (four to six pictures for each table). Also look for photographs that suggest themes, incidents, or settings related to the novel, such as mountain scenes, highways, rural living, families, couples, Appalachia, gardens, whirligigs, and holiday celebrations. Collect as many of these photographs as necessary for each group to have enough to assemble a collage measuring approximately 9-x-12 inches.

Photocopy Templates 7.5 through 7.7 onto construction paper. These templates will be used as bingo cards. There are six different cards; each of the six students at a table should have a different bingo card for the discussion game.

Base decorations on some significant setting or incident from the novel. Pictures or drawings of mountains could be used to re-create the location of Deep Water, West Virginia. The car trip to Putnam County could be suggested with maps, road signs, and outlines of cars on surrounding walls or partitions. The stop at Charleston at the Capitol Building could also be illustrated using drawings on wall murals. Much of the story takes place in Summer's trailer and the garden, both of which could be depicted using wall murals. Or, obtain brochures of the West Virginia Statehouse from the West Virginia Bureau of Tourism to use as table centerpieces or wall decorations. Whirligigs are available at many garden supply stores and can be placed in flowerpots on tables or around the room.

Student invitations to the program are written to mimic the tone and words of Ob's request to Cletus's parents to take him along on the trip (Template 7.3). These invitations can be delivered to students on the day of the program and can serve as their admission to the event.

Assemble the facilitators' packets, one for each table. Include a place card with the facilitator's name, a copy of the novel, the Agenda and Activity Instructions (Template 7.4), the Discussion Questions (Templates 7.8–7.9), and a thank-you note.

Confirm this list of materials needed for each table: facilitator's packet, four to six magazine photographs of older women, a game card (Templates 7.5–7.7) for each student, game tokens (these could be small pieces of paper or plastic), an assortment of magazine photographs for assembling a collage, a sheet of construction paper, and several glue sticks.

Whetting Their Appetite

Select one of these program ideas to prepare your students for the *Missing May* READ 'n' FEED program.

- Share one of the following picture books by Cynthia Rylant as a read-aloud: *When I Was Young in the Mountains, The Relatives Came, This Year's Garden,* or *The Blue Hill Meadows.* The first three of these books were adapted as filmstrips by Random House; you may prefer to use the filmstrip instead of reading the books aloud.

- Organize a booktalk program features other Cynthia Rylant young adult books: *A Couple of Kooks and Other Stories About Love, But I'll Be Back Again: An Album, I Had Seen Castles, A Kindness,* or *A Fine White Dust.* The booktalks could be written and presented by students.

- Adapt *Soda Jerk*, a group of narrative poems by Cynthia Rylant, into a readers theatre presentation. See *Readers Theatre for Young Adults: Scripts and Script Development* for an explanation of this process. Use student volunteers as the readers.

Mixing the Fiction, Food, and Fun

As students arrive, each is given a table assignment and a photograph clipped from a magazine. Facilitators at each table encourage each student to "tell the story" of the picture he or she has been given (as Cletus and Ob did in the novel). After this introductory activity, the facilitators explain the discussion format and pass out the game cards as the students begin eating. Each participant receives a bingo-like game card (Templates 7.5–7.7) and a small supply of "game tokens." There are six game card patterns; each student at a table should be given a different pattern to keep the game competitive. The facilitator begins the discussion game by asking a question from the list (Templates 7.8–7.9) of the student sitting to his or her left. Play continues around the table with each participant answering a question in turn. As the students answer the questions, the key words from the novel, which appear on the game card squares, should emerge as part of the discussion. When a student hears another student say a word that is on his or her card, the student may place a token on that square just as bingo is usually played. A student may place a token on the card when he or she hears another student say the word but not when he or she uses the word in answer to a question. If a word that a student "needs" is not mentioned, then he or she can design a question (related to *Missing May*) to elicit the needed word. The MISSING MAY square in the center of each card is a "free" square for all players. The object of the game is to be the first player to fill five squares in a row (horizontally, vertically, or diagonally) to score a bingo.

At the conclusion of the discussion game, facilitators lead the participants through an art activity. Each table receives glue sticks, thematic photographs clipped from magazines, and paper to serve as backing for a collage. The facilitator encourages the students to work together to create a collage expressing their views on the major theme(s) of the novel.

Hints for a Gourmet READ 'n' FEED

Set up a simple database report to make it easier for you to verify student participation and attendance, student homerooms, book circulation, and student testing results.

Plan at least 50 minutes to complete this program: 15 minutes for the introductory activity and food service, 20 minutes for the book discussion, and 15 minutes for the art activity.

Use an old valise to hold both the "story" photographs that are given to students as they arrive and the photographs that are used for the art activity.

Clip photographs of older women from magazines and place four to six of them on each table. The first discussion question asks students to describe how they think May looked and to select a photograph that most closely matches their impression of her. If time allows, give each student the opportunity to answer this question. It is a good idea to laminate these photographs as well as the game cards so that they can be used again.

Enhance the mood of the program by playing recorded mountain music as the students arrive and during the art activity.

Use the individual collages as pieces of a larger "patchwork quilt," which can be displayed in the library or media center to further promote the novel to the student body. Use a large sheet of bulletin board paper as the "backing" for the quilt. The student-made collages are the quilt patches or blocks. Smaller solid strips of construction paper (various colors) can be used as "fillers" between the collages.

Take photographs of the students attending the program and display the pictures along with the quilt collage. You can use the photographs as part of your publicity effort the next time *Missing May* is the selected READ 'n' FEED novel.

Novel Connections

Select one or more of these follow-up activities to extend READ 'n' FEED program.

- Record volunteer hours of READ 'n' FEED participants at senior centers or nursing homes.
- Present information to students about the various worldwide child-relief agencies that provide funding to support the needs of children.
- Contact a counselor or member of a grief support group to share information with the students about grieving.

More Book Bites

Hite, Sid. *It's Nothing to a Mountain.* New York: Henry Holt, 1994.

Hosie-Bounar, Jane. *Life Belts.* New York: Delacorte Press, 1993.

Irwin, Hadley. *So Long at the Fair.* New York: Margaret K. McElderry, 1988.

MacLachlan, Patricia. *Baby.* New York: Delacorte Press, 1993.

Mazer, Norma Fox. *After the Rain.* New York: William Morrow, 1987.

Paterson, Katherine. *Flip-Flop Girl.* New York: E. P. Dutton, 1994.

Templates

Publicity Poster, Template 7.1

Flush Flash, Template 7.2

Student Invitation, Template 7.3

Agenda and Activity Instructions, Template 7.4

Game Cards; Template 7.5

Game Cards, Template 7.6

Game Cards, Template 7.7

Discussion Questions, Template 7.8

Discussion Questions, Template 7.9

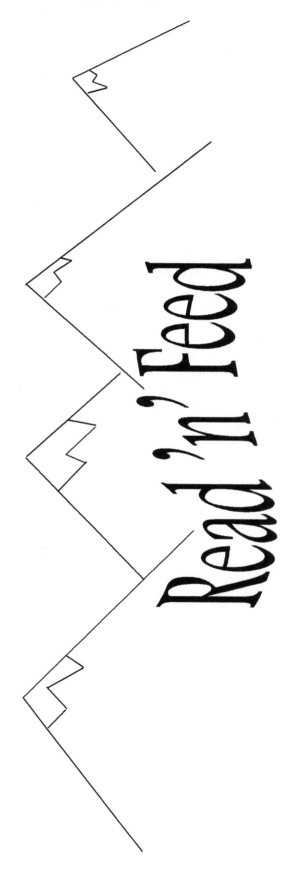

Read 'n' Feed

Sign up! Sign up today! Don't miss getting a copy of the book! Sign up! Sign up today!

Fiction: MISSING MAY
by Cynthia Rylant

Date:

Time:

Food:

Fun: It will turn your buggy around!

Place:

Template 7.1. Publicity Poster.

MISSING MAY

by Cynthia Rylant

Winner of the 1993 Newbery Award

Did you know that Cynthia Rylant got her first kiss when she was 11 years old, and "for the next several years I did so much kissing that I barely had time to take a breath. I loved to kiss, and still do, and apart from going out for ice cream, there are few things as easy and enjoyable."

from *But I'll Be Back Again: An Album*
by Cynthia Rylant

Find out where Summer's search for May takes her. Sign up to read *Missing May* by Cynthia Rylant. Be there! Don't MISS it! No MISSING!

When you read, we feed!!

Date:

Meet CLETUS, a former collector of potato chip bags, who has been called a FLAT OUT LUNATIC.

Of course everyone is MISSING MAY, "she was a big barrel of nothing but love . . .she had faith in every single person she ever met. Seems people knew she saw the very best of them, and they'd turn that side to her to give her a better look."

Sign up and pick up a book:

For more information, contact:

What do you call a tiny fortune-teller who has escaped from jail?
A small medium at large!

Template 7.2. Flush Flash.

From *Fiction, Food, and Fun.* © 1998. Closter, Sipes, Thomas. Libraries Unlimited. (800) 237-6124.

We were wondering if
you might like to take
a little trip with us to
visit an old friend down
in Putnam County. We
will probably do a little
sightseeing along the way.
Can you come?
We'll be MISSING MAY

_____
(date)

_____
(time)

_____
(location)

We were wondering if
you might like to take
a little trip with us to
visit an old friend down
in Putnam County. We
will probably do a little
sightseeing along the way.
Can you come?
We'll be MISSING MAY

_____
(date)

_____
(time)

_____
(location)

We were wondering if
you might like to take
a little trip with us to
visit an old friend down
in Putnam County. We
will probably do a little
sightseeing along the way.
Can you come?
We'll be MISSING MAY

_____
(date)

_____
(time)

_____
(location)

We were wondering if
you might like to take
a little trip with us to
visit an old friend down
in Putnam County. We
will probably do a little
sightseeing along the way.
Can you come?
We'll be MISSING MAY

_____
(date)

_____
(time)

_____
(location)

Template 7.3. Student Invitation.

READ 'n' FEED
Missing May

AGENDA

_____ (10 min.)   Students receive seating assignments and meal; begin eating

_____ (5 min.)   Introductions
Ask each student to introduce himself or herself and to "tell the story" of the picture he or she received upon arrival (as Cletus and Ob did in the novel).

_____ (2 min.)   Explanation of discussion format and game

_____ (20 min.)   Book discussion

_____ (15 min.)   Art activity

Activity Instructions

Explain that the discussion of the novel will take place while playing a bingo-like game. Each player should have a game card and a small supply of game tokens.

Begin by asking the student on your left the first question from the list of discussion questions. If time allows, all the players should answer the first question. Play continues around the table with each player answering questions in turn. As questions are answered, key words from the novel, which fill the game card spaces, should emerge as part of the discussion. When a player hears another player say a word which is on his or her card, he or she may place a token on that square just as bingo is usually played. A player may place a token on the card when he or she hears another player say the word but not when he or she uses the word in answer to a question. If a word a player "needs" is not mentioned, he or she may design a question (related to *Missing May*) to elicit the needed word.

The MISSING MAY square in the center of each card is a "free" square for all players. The object of the game is to be the first player to fill five squares in a row (horizontally, vertically, or diagonally) to score a "bingo."

Template 7.4. Agenda and Activity Instructions.

whirligigs	Cletus	suitcase	Coke	Newbery
Valiant	chocolate milk	Cynthia	Ohio	mountains
writer	miracle	MISSING MAY	oversleep	coffee shop
bats	relatives	Thanksgiving	flood	trailer
afterlife	brochure	Deep Water	school bus	love

Thanksgiving	trip	Cynthia	gold dome	Summer
TV dinner	Ohio	capitol	oversleep	angels
Phyllis Whitney	coffee shop	MISSING MAY	funeral	Putnam County
West Virginia	trailer	cry	mountains	love
heaven	garden	Coke	flood	Newbery

Template 7.5. Game Cards.

afterlife	Ob	bats	home	writer
Charleston	Valiant	Oz	whirligigs	spiritualist
brochure	Christmas	MISSING MAY	relatives	cocoa
miracle	earflaps	owl	Deep Water	Rylant
school bus	garden	flood	death	suitcase

Putnam County	cry	heaven	Phyllis Whitney	capitol
Summer	whirligigs	old Chevy	chocolate milk	pictures
flood	breakfast	MISSING MAY	washtub	love
trailer	coffee	Newbery	surreal	mountains
West Virginia	Coke	funeral	suitcase	angels

Template 7.6. Game Cards.

spiritualist	garden	gold dome	TV dinner	coffee
Oz	Rylant	trip	angels	washtub
Charleston	earflaps	MISSING MAY	funeral	breakfast
home	cocoa	death	West Virginia	pictures
Ob	Christmas	owl	surreal	old Chevy

washtub	breakfast	pictures	Cletus	old Chevy
family	owl	angels	home	chocolate milk
Deep Water	school bus	MISSING MAY	capitol	trip
spiritualist	relatives	writer	brochure	Thanksgiving
gold dome	Rylant	oversleep	miracle	death

Template 7.7. Game Cards.

MISSING MAY

Facilitator's Guide
Discussion Questions
(Page numbers refer to the Dell paperback edition of *Missing May*.)

1. Describe how you think May looked. Do you think she resembled any of the photographs on the table?

2. How does Summer describe May? (pp. 15-16)

3. What do you think Ob's whirligigs looked like? What were some of them called? (pp. 6-7)

4. What did Summer mean when she said she "felt like a magical little girl, a chosen little girl, like Alice who has fallen into Wonderland?" (p. 7)

5. What does Summer think of Cletus Underwood when he first starts coming to the trailer? (pp. 19-24)

6. How and why does Summer's relationship with Cletus change?

7. What is Ob's relationship with Cletus?

8. What were Ob, Cletus, and Summer doing in the garden (front cover)? Whose idea was it? What did Summer think about it?

9. Why did Ob think that Cletus could talk to May? (p. 30)

10. Why does Summer fear losing Ob? (pp. 30-31)

11. Summer speaks of the denouement occurring in their story. When was that? What importance did it have to their story? (p. 43)

12. How did Summer feel on the day her fourth-grade classmate wrote a description of her? How does she see herself? (p. 46)

13. What does Summer think is the reason Ob overslept and did not get dressed when he did get up? (p. 47)

MISSING MAY

Template 7.8. Discussion Questions.

From *Fiction, Food, and Fun.* © 1998. Closter, Sipes, Thomas. Libraries Unlimited. (800) 237-6124.

MISSING MAY

Facilitator's Guide
Discussion Questions

(Page numbers refer to the Dell paperback edition of *Missing May*.)

14. Why is Summer willing to go see the spiritualist with Ob and Cletus if she thinks it's such a crazy idea? (p. 54)

15. What does Summer mean when she says she has "too much to lose if this Bat Lady turns out to be a hoax"? (p. 56)

16. Summer sees similarities in their journey to the journey taken to Oz by Dorothy and her friends. What are the similarities? (pp. 43, 71)

17. What does Summer learn about Cletus's life when she and Ob go to his house? (pp. 60-61)

18. How is the silence on the way home from Putnam County different from the silence on the way to Putnam County? (p. 76)

19. What do you think happened to Ob after he left the spiritualist's house that made him want "to turn that buggy around"? (p. 80)

20. How does the owl flying over affect Summer?

21. How does Ob change through the story? How does Summer change through the story? Does Cletus change?

22. What is the theme or message of this story?

23. Is the setting important to the story? Is the time or year important? What does the garden symbolize?

24. What do you think of the title?

25. Do you think the author tells us enough about May for us to care about her?

26. How would you describe this book to a friend?

MISSING MAY

Template 7.9. Discussion Questions.

From *Fiction, Food, and Fun.* © 1998. Closter, Sipes, Thomas. Libraries Unlimited. (800) 237-6124.

Chapter 8

The Silver Kiss

Bibliographic Information

Annette Curtis Klause. *The Silver Kiss*. Delacorte Press, 1990. 198 pages. $3.50. ISBN 0-440-421346-0.

Interest Level

Grades 7 through 10

Themes

Relationships, Friendship, Death

Plot Summary

Zoë despairs over her mother's illness, the lack of attention from her father, and a friend's move to Oregon . . . until she meets Simon. One kiss, a silver kiss, from Simon will make Zoë belong to him forever in this young adult vampire story.

Author Information

Writing a vampire story was something that Annette Curtis Klause could really sink her teeth into. As a child, she spent hours listening to her father tell spooky, spine-tingling stories and describe grisly movie plots. Before long, she was writing her own stories just for fun. She was born in Bristol, England, in 1953, and her family moved to Washington, D.C., when she was a teenager. She continued to write, but it wasn't until she graduated from college and began her career as a librarian that she submitted her first novel for publication. The poems and prose she wrote as a teenager while in the throes of a vampire obsession she now calls "dreadful," although they proved useful when she started to write *The Silver Kiss*. Klause remembers reading her first vampire novel—*The Shiny Narrow Grin* by Jane Gaskell—when she was 14 years old. She credits it as her inspiration

157

for *The Silver Kiss,* which won the ALA Best Books for Young Adults award in 1990 and the *School Library Journal* Best Book award in 1991. Her second novel, *Alien Secrets,* was an ALA Notable Book, *School Library Journal* Best Book, *Booklist* Editor's Choice, and *New York Public Library Journal* Best Book, all in 1993.

Booktalk

It seemed as though everyone was leaving Zoë. Her mother was slowly dying of cancer; her father's concern for his wife had made him all but forget he had a daughter; now Lorraine, her best friend, was moving to Oregon. Then Simon came into her life. She saw him late one moonlit night in the park as she sat brooding about her circumstances. He came stealthily, like a shadow, and for a moment they held each other's gaze. His eyes were dark, full of wilderness and stars. With a sudden ache, she realized he was beautiful. He saw something in her that made him remember what it felt like to be alive, and he wanted more.

Zoë is apprehensive when Simon comes to her house, but there is something soothing in him that persuades her to invite him inside. Simon seems to understand the pain of loneliness and death, and Zoë's brooding thoughts of her dying mother.

Sitting close to Zoë, Simon begins to talk about himself. He, too, often thinks of death, for he is one of the undead. Centuries before, his brother cruelly murdered their mother and made Simon a vampire. Now, he wants revenge. Simon is amazed that he is telling Zoë this. He doesn't talk much to people—they're just food. He'd spent years thinking of people as mindless, stupid creatures unfit to live. That way of thinking made it easier for him to use them; now he was letting one become real to him. He knows he must be detached to survive, but he wants to be with this girl, talk with her, maybe even give her a kiss—the silver kiss, the one that could make her his forever.

What's Cookin' at the READ 'n' FEED?

Zoë is despaired over her mother's illness, the lack of attention from her father, and a friend's move to Oregon . . . until she meets Simon. One kiss from Simon, the *silver kiss*, will make her belong to Simon forever. Silver kisses, coffins, and rats draw students into the vampire myth as they play a "Win, Lose, or Draw" game illustrating terms from the novel. The first student at the table to guess the term gets a chocolate kiss. Students discuss the significance of the term to the story and receive tokens for their answers that can be redeemed for prizes. Locating the event in a place that gives the effect of being a dirty, abandoned school basement enhances this READ 'n' FEED. The use of the color silver, stamped "kisses," and red puff paint create an atmosphere of ghoulish excitement.

Preparations

Read "The Recipe for a Successful READ 'n' FEED Program" at the beginning of this book for a discussion of those materials, designs, resources, and handouts needed for every READ 'n' FEED. Be sure to copy the Planning Outline and Program Checklist form in the appendix of this book, so you will have it ready for your first design team meeting. In addition, this program requires props suggestive of vampires, drawing easels, markers, tokens of different values, and chocolate kisses.

SHOPPING LIST

- Empty cylindrically shaped cans like those in which tennis balls are packaged; one for each table
- Aluminum foil
- Markers and small drawing easels or small white boards with dry erase markers; one for each table
- Spooky music
- Red lightbulbs
- Table coverings, plates, napkins, cups, dinnerware as needed
- Materials for decorations: plastic rats, stuffed teddy bear, coffin, skeleton, cobwebs, old suitcase, black leather jacket
- Red puff paint
- Construction paper: red, black
- Chocolate kisses
- A "lip"-shaped stamp and ink pad

ADDING THE GARNISHES

- Concrete Blonde. "Bloodletting," I.R.S. IRSD-82037, 1990 (CD).
- Cremer, Robert. *Lugosi: The Man Behind the Cape.* Chicago: Henry Regnery, 1976.
- Nightmare Factory, P.O. Box 1181, Dripping Springs, Texas 78620, (512) 858-5063 (fax); Web site: http://www.nightmarefactory.com/
- Rainy, Richard. *The Monster Factor.* New York: New Discovery Books, 1993.

FOOD FOR THOUGHT

Tuna casserole, cereal, and rat's blood are foods mentioned in the book. But seeing as vampires won't be invited to your event, spaghetti, breadsticks, and dirt pudding garnished with gummy bears make a great menu. (See Template 8.9 for a recipe for dirt pudding.)

WHIPPING UP THE FUN

Publicize the program. Copy the publicity poster (Template 8.1) and the Flush Flash (Template 8.2). Add local event details before displaying these promotional templates. Write a student announcement using the sample from the "Booktalk" section of this chapter. Distribute books to the students with a schedule of event dates and expectation deadlines. (See the sample Student Time Line Memo in the appendix at the end of this book.)

Select facilitators and give each of them a copy of the novel to read. At least a week before the program, supply the facilitators with any special instructions, Agenda and Activity Instructions (Templates 8.4a and 8.4b), the "BLOOD DRAW" terms (Templates 8.5a and 8.5b) and the Dirt Pudding Recipe (Template 8.9).

Plan decorations. Our school's unfinished basement was the perfect setting for this program as it looked exactly like the abandoned school in which Simon hid during the day. Many schools may not have access to such a basement. If not, borrow a casket from a local funeral home, add a human skeleton borrowed from the science department, a few battery-operated candles, black table coverings, a couple of plastic rats, a teddy bear, cobwebs, a black leather jacket, mood music, and voilà! You have created an atmosphere fit for Count Dracula himself. Ask facilitators to wear black; better yet, invite them to don capes, makeup, and vampire teeth. If you use black paper to cover the tables, drip spots of red puff paint on it for decoration.

To make the containers for the "BLOOD DRAW" game, cover the cylinder-shaped cans with aluminum. Copy as many of the "BLOOD DRAW" terms (Template 8.5a and 8.5b) as you need on red construction paper, laminate the sheets, and cut them into long strips, one term per strip. Put these strips into the silver cans. Decorate the top of each canister with red puff paint. Use the puff paint to label the canisters with the words "BLOOD DRAW." Copy the "10 points" tokens (Template 8.6) and the "20 points" tokens (Template 8.7) on red paper. Laminate the sheets, cut the tokens, and place these in a small container.

You will need one can of BLOOD DRAW strips, a marker, a drawing pad, 10- and 20-point tokens, and a container of chocolate kisses for each table.

Prepare a drawing easel, a description of which is included in Chapter 6, *"Maniac Magee,"* under the section, "Hints for a Gourmet READ 'n' FEED." Staple 25 sheets of white paper to each easel.

Copy the invitation (Template 8.3). Deliver these to students who qualify to attend. This is the student's ticket. Copy the Seating Place Cards sheets (Template 8.8) and write the names of the participants on the cards with red puff paint. If you were able to find a "lip" stamp, you can also decorate the place cards with red lips. Ask facilitators to contribute a batch of dirt pudding (Template 8.9) and serve it up in clear plastic cups with gummy bear garnish. This should stimulate a discussion of what the bear with the dirt inside represents to the vampire Chris.

Assemble the facilitator's packets. Each packet should include a place card with the facilitator's name, a copy of the novel, the Agenda and Activity Instruction, and a thank-you note. Place a packet at each table.

Whetting Their Appetite

Select one of these program ideas to prepare the students for the READ 'n' FEED program.

- Present a vampire make-up demonstration.
- Booktalk other books of the same genre.
- Research and share gruesome facts behind the vampire myths.
- Gather some fun facts about the vampire myths and show a short segment of Bela Lugosi's *Count Dracula.*

Mixing the Fiction, Food, and Fun

Create an atmosphere in which a vampire would feel at home. Play spooky music as the students check in; try "Bloodletting (The Vampire Song)" by Concrete Blonde. Then students pick up their food and find their seats. "BLOOD DRAW" is played at each table. Play begins as one player pulls a "BLOOD DRAW" word slip from the silver canister. The word is shown only to the facilitator. Next, the player attempts to draw the item and elicit a response from the group. The first person to guess the word correctly gets a chocolate kiss and a 10-point token from the facilitator, who then proceeds to ask the student to define or explain the significance of the term in the novel. If the player answers to the satisfaction of the facilitator, he or she is given a 20-point token. Continue play around the table so that everyone has a chance to draw. The person with the highest number of points at the end of the game wins. It is nice to have prizes for the winner at each table. Reading motivation T-shirts, related paperback books, Annette Curtis Klause's *Alien Secrets,* or a gift certificate to a local bookstore are all appropriate.

Hints for a Gourmet READ 'n' FEED

Set up a simple database report to make it easier for you to verify student participation and attendance, student homerooms, book circulation, and student testing results.

The atmosphere and costuming for this book lend themselves to creativity and fun. Take extra pains in planning this program, and the students will respond enthusiastically. The music you choose to set the mood can vary from classical to rock.

Make sure you allow enough drying time for the puff paint—at least 24 hours.

Don't forget to evaluate your program. Student and facilitator comments will help you revise and adjust future READ 'n' FEED programs. A sample evaluation form is included in the appendix at the end of this book.

Novel Connections

- Compose a song lyric that would fit the title "I Got the Vampire Blues."
- Write a poem, from Zoë's point of view, about Simon.
- Find out if your community has a support group for teens who have a terminally ill parent. If so, make that information available at your school. If not, find out how to start one.

More Book Bites

Cusick, Richie Tankersley. *Buffy, the Vampire Slayer.* New York: Pocket Books, 1992.

———. *Vampire.* New York: Pocket Books, 1991.

Garden, Nancy. *My Sister, the Vampire.* New York: Alfred A. Knopf, 1992.

———. *Prisoner of Vampires.* New York: Dell, 1986.

Hambly, Barbara. *Those Who Hunt the Night.* New York: Ballantine Books, 1988.

Huff, Tanya. *Blood Price.* New York: DAW Books, 1991.

Lichtenburg, Jacqueline. *Those of My Blood.* New York: St. Martin's Press, 1988.

Lykken, Laurie. *Little Room of Terror.* Pinellas Park, FL: Willowisp Press, 1991.

Rice, Anne. *Interview with the Vampire.* New York: Ballantine Books, 1977.

Stine, R. L. *Goodnight Kiss.* New York: Pocket Books, 1992.

Stoker, Bram. *Dracula*. New York: Dell, 1972.

Yolen, Jane, and Martin H. Greenberg, eds. *Vampires: A Collection of Original Stories*. New York: HarperCollins, 1991.

Templates

Publicity Poster, Template 8.1

Flush Flash, Template 8.2

Invitation, Template 8.3

Agenda and Activity Instructions, Template 8.4a and 8.4b

"BLOOD DRAW" Terms, Template 8.5a and 8.5b

10-Points Tokens, Template 8.6

20-Points Tokens, Template 8.7

Seating Place Cards, Template 8.8

Dirt Pudding Recipe, Template 8.9

READ 'n' FEED

SIGN UP FOR YOUR COPY

READ IT!

PROVE IT!

ENJOY THE FUN!

Template 8.1. Publicity Poster.

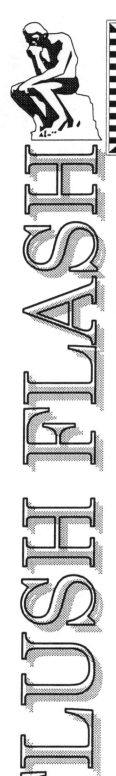

The Silver Kiss

Date:

by Annette Curtis Klause

Vampire Trivia

Did you know that vampires:

-cannot cross a threshold unless they are invited?
-must have consecrated soil from their native land in order to rest?
-can be destroyed if a wooden stake is driven through their heart?
-cannot survive in sunlight?
-cannot harm a person who is wearing a crucifix?
-cannot harm a person who is wearing a necklace made of garlic?
-can turn themselves into other shapes?

KLAUSE'S FIRST NOVEL

Annette Curtis Klause's first novel, *The Silver Kiss* is a gothic romance for young adults. It is told from the point of view of two characters: Zoë and Simon. Zoë is a teenager whose world is crumbling. Simon is a 300 year-old teenage vampire. When they see each other in the park late one night, they discover that they both have something the other one needs. Check it out! See your librarian today!

Questions

Who was Bela Lugosi?

What is a lamia in Greek mythology?

Who is Bram Stoker?

Who was Count Dracula?

Is Transylvania a real place?

Who was Vlad the Impaler?

What is a gothic novel?

Answers

Now you didn't think it would be that easy, did you? The answers are found in the library, or on the World Wide Web, or in a dictionary, or in your teachers' heads. See how many answers you can find.

Sponsored by

Template 8.2. Flush Flash.

Zoe,

Meet me in the library

S

The Silver Kiss
READ 'n' FEED

To _____
Date _____
Time _____
Place _____
RSVP _____

◆

Template 8.3. Invitation.

READ 'n' FEED

The Silver Kiss

Agenda

_____	(10 min.)	Serve and seat participants; begin eating
_____	(20 min.)	Play "BLOOD DRAW"
_____	(5 min.)	Tally points
_____	(5 min.)	Award prizes to winners

BLOOD DRAW

Object of the game: Collect the most chocolate kisses (or points) by the end of the game. *Facilitator: You may want to explain to your table that " BLOOD DRAW" is a game similar to the game "Win, Lose, or Draw." Read the directions aloud. For the Novel Connections phase of the game, reward specific names or examples. Vague answers do not get points. Some possible questions and responses are listed here.*

Directions: Play begins with the youngest player at the table, who selects a word out of the silver canister. The player attempts to draw symbols for that term while the others at the table try to guess the term. The first student to guess gets a token worth 10 points (or a chocolate kiss). That winning student then has the opportunity to make a "Novel Connection" by answering: *1– What significance does this word have in the novel? or 2– Tell us of some important event connecting this word with the story.* If you feel that the student has answered the question with a concrete connection to the book, you can give that student a token worth 20 points (or two chocolate kisses). Continue around the table so that everyone has a chance to draw a term at least once. The student with the highest number of points at the end of the game wins a prize.

Novel Connections

Death: Explain any aspect of death as portrayed in the novel. (Several people are murdered in the novel, Zoë's mother is dying, Simon and Zoë are afraid of death.)
Silver: Explain why the word *silver* is so important to the book's title. (The author uses this color throughout the novel to describe the color of Simon's hair, the moonlight, and the crucifix that Lorraine gives to Zoë.)
Christopher: Explain how Christopher became a vampire, or how he treats his victims. Explain why he treats them in such a harsh, cruel way. Describe how he lures his victims before he kills them.
Zoe: Zoë is drawn to Simon. She thinks Simon is beautiful even though she is afraid of him. What do they have in common? (Zoë helps Simon feel as if he belongs somewhere.)

Template 8.4a. Agenda and Activity Instructions.

READ 'n' FEED

The Silver Kiss

BLOOD DRAW

Novel Connections
(continued from Template 8.4a)

Lorraine: How does Lorraine fit into this novel? (She is moving away, so Zoë has to come to grips with another separation besides that resulting from her mother's impending death. Lorraine gives Zoë the crucifix, which eventually aids in the destruction of Christopher.)

Simon: Describe his beauty, his sensitivity to Zoë's pain in trying to deal with her mother's cancer. Explain how Simon became a vampire. How does he sustain his existence, in contrast to Christopher's methods? How does he feel about his brother?

Fear: Fear of death is a central theme in the novel. Explain how fear was the thing that caused Simon and Zoë to be drawn to each other. Cite other examples of fear from the novel.

Hospital: What is the significance of the hospital? (Zoë's mother is in the hospital. Zoë is angry about not being allowed to visit her mother as often as she would like. Zoë takes Simon with her to visit her mother.)

Local park bench: What is the significance of the park bench? (It is the place where Zoë first saw Simon. She feels angry for being disturbed. This is also the location of Christopher's eventual death, and the last place Zoë sees Simon before he vaporizes.)

Alley: What is the significance of the alley? (Zoë sees Christopher in the alley. She sees Simon eating a dead bird, and she sees a victim of a murder in the alley. This is also the place where Simon says to her, "It's death.")

Wulfram Von Crab: Describe his cruelty to Christopher and Simon. Describe how he lures his victims.

Soil: What is the signficance of the soil that is found in Christopher's bear and Simon's suitcase? (The vampires' survival depends upon having the soil.)

Poetry: Zoë likes to write poetry. (She wrote a poem about Simon.)

Rats: Explain how Simon uses rats. (Simon feeds on rats instead of humans.)

Teddy Bear: Describe how Christopher uses his teddy bear. (He keeps his soil in the bear.)

Abandoned School: What is the significance of the abandoned school? (This is where Simon sleeps during the daylight hours.)

Vampires: Describe some characteristics common to all vampires. (They all need soil to survive. They can be destroyed by a stake through the heart. Sunlight can destroy them.)

Crucifix: Describe the significance of the necklace that Zoë's friend, Lorraine, gave to her. (It was a crucifix. A crucifix is supposed to keep vampires away. The necklace saved Zoë from harm.)

Template 8.4b. Agenda and Activity Instructions.

SIMON	CHRISTOPHER	TEDDY BEAR	PARK BENCH	FEAR	HOSPITAL	CRUCIFIX	VAMPIRES	ABANDONED SCHOOL

Template 8.5a. "BLOOD DRAW" Terms.

WULFRAM VON CRAB							
SOIL	POETRY	RATS	ZOË	DEATH	SILVER	ALLEY	LORRAINE

Template 8.5b. "BLOOD DRAW" Terms.

10 POINTS
BLOOD DRAW

10 POINTS
BLOOD DRAW

10 POINTS
BLOOD DRAW

10 POINTS
BLOOD DRAW

10 POINTS
BLOOD DRAW

10 POINTS
BLOOD DRAW

10 POINTS
BLOOD DRAW

10 POINTS
BLOOD DRAW

10 POINTS
BLOOD DRAW

10 POINTS
BLOOD DRAW

Template 8.6. 10-Points Tokens.

20 POINTS

BLOOD DRAW

20 POINTS

BLOOD DRAW

20 POINTS

BLOOD DRAW

20 POINTS

BLOOD DRAW

20 POINTS

BLOOD DRAW

20 POINTS

BLOOD DRAW

20 POINTS

BLOOD DRAW

20 POINTS

BLOOD DRAW

20 POINTS

BLOOD DRAW

20 POINTS

BLOOD DRAW

Template 8.7. 20-Points Tokens.

Reserved for

Reserved for

Reserved for

Reserved for

Reserved for

Reserved for

Reserved for

Reserved for

Reserved for

Reserved for

Reserved for

Reserved for

Template 8.8. Seating Place Cards.

Dirt Dessert with Gummy Bears

2 packages Oreo cookies, crushed
9 ounce-packaged instant vanilla pudding
1 tub Cool Whip whipped topping

Blend cookies in a blender and set aside. Prepare pudding with 1/2 the milk called for on the box. After the pudding has set, fold in Cool Whip. Alternate layers of cookie crumbs and pudding mixure in a 9- x- 13 inch pan. Make sure you leave enough cookie crumbs to cover the top. Garnish with gummy bears. Serve in individual clear plastic cups at the READ 'n' FEED.

Dirt Dessert with Gummy Bears

2 packages Oreo cookies, crushed
9 ounce-packaged instant vanilla pudding
1 tub Cool Whip whipped topping

Blend cookies in a blender and set aside. Prepare pudding with 1/2 the milk called for on the box. After the pudding has set, fold in Cool Whip. Alternate layers of cookie crumbs and pudding mixure in a 9- x- 13 inch pan. Make sure you leave enough cookie crumbs to cover the top. Garnish with gummy bears. Serve in individual clear plastic cups at the READ 'n' FEED.

Dirt Dessert with Gummy Bears

2 packages Oreo cookies, crushed
9 ounce-packaged instant vanilla pudding
1 tub Cool Whip whipped topping

Blend cookies in a blender and set aside. Prepare pudding with 1/2 the milk called for on the box. After the pudding has set, fold in Cool Whip. Alternate layers of cookie crumbs and pudding mixure in a 9- x- 13 inch pan. Make sure you leave enough cookie crumbs to cover the top. Garnish with gummy bears. Serve in individual clear plastic cups at the READ 'n' FEED.

Dirt Dessert with Gummy Bears

2 packages Oreo cookies, crushed
9 ounce-packaged instant vanilla pudding
1 tub Cool Whip whipped topping

Blend cookies in a blender and set aside. Prepare pudding with 1/2 the milk called for on the box. After the pudding has set, fold in Cool Whip. Alternate layers of cookie crumbs and pudding mixure in a 9- x- 13 inch pan. Make sure you leave enough cookie crumbs to cover the top. Garnish with gummy bears. Serve in individual clear plastic cups at the READ 'n' FEED.

Template 8.9. Dirt Pudding Recipe.

From *Fiction, Food, and Fun.* © 1998. Closter, Sipes, Thomas. Libraries Unlimited. (800) 237-6124.

Chapter **9**

The Trouble with Lemons

Bibliographic Information

Daniel Hayes. *The Trouble with Lemons*. New York: Fawcett Juniper, 1991. 187 pages. $3.99. ISBN 0-449-70416-5.

Interest Level

Grades 7 through 9

Themes

Friendship, Self-Esteem, Personal Relationships, Truth, Compassion

Plot Summary

Tyler and Lymie, eighth grade misfits, discover a dead body in a quarry and work to uncover the mystery behind it.

Author Information

Daniel Hayes has created a memorable character in Tyler McAllister, featured in *The Trouble with Lemons, Eye of the Beholder,* and *No Effect.* All three of these books have been well received, earning two ALA Best Books for Young Adults awards for Hayes. Tyler's popularity with young adults lies in his authenticity and humor. Hayes has said that his friends recognize him in the voice and character of Tyler, and he feels that his characters reflect his many different sides.

Daniel Hayes began planning a writing career when he rediscovered books such as *The Adventures of Huckleberry Finn* and *Great Expectations* while in college. Those books inspired him to study the works of Mark Twain, Charles Dickens, and other writers and to begin the search for his own voice and style. He enjoys writing and has said that "the difference I found with this thing was that I didn't have the feeling I was constantly swimming against the current." Hayes plans on writing more books featuring Tyler and his pal Lymie, much to the delight of his fans.

Booktalk

Meet Tyler McAllister, who calls himself a lemon. Lemon? Like the little yellow fruit, lemon? Not exactly. Tyler thinks he's a lemon as in lemon, a screw-up, a defective product. And to make matters worse, he's starting the school year at a new school. He's sure everyone thinks he's weird and sees that he is, indeed, a lemon. He manages to make friends with a kid named Lymie, though, so things start to look a little more promising to him. That feeling lasts about a week. Right up until the night he and Lymie go skinny-dipping at the quarry. Tyler is just floating around when he suddenly feels something sliding down his back. He prays that it is a big friendly fish swimming by. When he turns around to look, he freaks! He is staring at a face, pale and bloated. And hands, slimy hands, reaching for his throat! A dead body! All his old problems suddenly seem minor compared with this new problem. You see, he and Lymie saw two shadowy figures leaving the quarry in a big hurry. Were they murderers, dropping the body? Would they now be after Tyler and Lymie? Read *The Trouble with Lemons* by Daniel Hayes to find out!

What's Cookin' at the READ 'n' FEED?

The program for this novel uses a board game that facilitates a discussion of the events of the story and the feelings of the main character. The game board is designed in the shape of a wheel with an outer circle, spokes, and a hub. Students take turns rolling a die and moving board markers around the outer circle initially. Each move requires an answer to a question about the novel. The students then position their markers to proceed along a spoke toward the center of the wheel. Each spoke represents a different component of the concept of self-esteem. As the students move their markers along the spokes, they relate the self-esteem concepts to incidents in the novel, specifically, incidents relating to the main character's developing self-esteem. Following the discussion, booktalks about the sequels to this novel inspire students to read more books by author Daniel Hayes.

Preparations

Check "The Recipe for a Successful READ 'n' FEED Program" at the beginning of this book for a discussion of those materials, designs, resources, and handouts needed for every READ 'n' FEED program. Be sure to copy the Planning Outline and Program Checklist form in the appendix of this book so you will have it ready for your first design team meeting. In addition, this program will require a game board, board markers, game cards, and a die for each table.

SHOPPING LIST

- 18-x-18-inch squares of colored paper
- Construction paper: bright yellow
- Felt-tipped markers in eight different colors
- Dice
- Small pieces of paper or plastic to use as board markers
- Table coverings, plates, napkins, cups, dinnerware as needed

- Lemon-scented air freshener
- Materials for decoration: lemons (real, plastic, or paper) and posters with positive self-esteem messages

ADDING THE GARNISHES

- Ask the school librarian or the Young Adult librarian at the local public library to prepare a bibliography on the subject of self-esteem.
- Offer the students the opportunity to review some of the many personality or interest quizzes found in popular teen magazines.

FOOD FOR THOUGHT

There aren't many foods mentioned in this novel, so you may want to select a menu that features foods popular with your students. The foods that are mentioned include eggs, fried chicken, hamburgers, canned spaghetti, and ice cream. Be sure to include something containing lemon, perhaps lemon meringue pie, lemon bars, lemon candy, tea with lemon, fish with lemon, lemon soda, lemon cookies, or lemon cake.

WHIPPING UP THE FUN

Publicize the program at least a month in advance. Copy the Publicity Poster (Template 9.1) and Flush Flash (Template 9.2). Add your own local event details before displaying these templates. Write a promotional announcement for your school's daily announcements, calendar of events, or newspaper using the "Booktalk" or "Plot Summary" sections of this chapter. Distribute the books to the students along with information about the date of the program and any participation requirements. (See the sample Student Time Line Memo in the appendix at the end of this book.)

Select facilitators and give each one a copy of the novel to read. At least a week before the program, supply the facilitators with any special instructions, an Agenda and Activity Instruction guide (Template 9.4), and the discussion questions (Templates 9.10–9.12).

The game boards for "LEMON SHAKE-UP" are easily made using a piece of 18-x-18-inch colored paper onto which is glued a large paper "wheel" with spokes and a hub. Draw two large circles on white paper; one inside the other to create the wheel. The outside circle should have a diameter of approximately 16 inches and the inner circle a diameter of approximately 14.5 inches. Mark off equal sections of approximately 1.5 inches all the way around the wheel by drawing a series of lines across the space between the outer circle and the inner circle. Color the sections with markers using eight colors, one color per section. Repeat the pattern of eight colors around the entire wheel. Cut out the finished wheel and glue it to the large square of colored paper.

Create the spokes for the wheel by cutting eight rectangles approximately one inch by seven inches out of white paper. Draw a series of horizontal lines, one every .75 inches, across the width of each rectangle. All eight rectangles, or spokes, should then be colored. Use the eight markers to color each spoke a different color (all the sections of each spoke will be the same color). Use a black marker to write the following concepts on the spokes (one concept per spoke): DEVELOP YOUR OWN VALUES, DON'T BE AFRAID TO TAKE RISKS, TURN SETBACKS INTO VICTORIES, DEMAND RESPECT FROM OTHERS, SEEK FULFILLING RELATIONSHIPS, ACCEPT WHO YOU ARE, AVOID BEING JUDGMENTAL, and GIVE YOURSELF CREDIT. Cut out the spokes and glue them in place within the wheel on the colored square. The spokes should be arranged equidistant from each other in a pattern that radiates from the center of the space within the wheel.

The hub or center is a circle approximately three inches in diameter; it should be colored with some color other than the eight already used. Use a black marker to write the term SELF-ESTEEM on the hub. Cut out the hub and glue it to the center of the intersection of the spokes. If you prefer, create the game board using colored paper, a label maker, and a desktop publishing program rather than white paper, markers, and hand lettering. The final product should be a large square with a multicolored wheel, eight differently colored spokes, and a hub.

Prepare one set of "LEMON SHAKE-UP" game cards for each discussion table. Copy the "LEMON SHAKE-UP" game card backs (Template 9.5) onto one side of four sheets of bright yellow construction paper. Be sure to trim the width of the construction paper to equal the width of the original copy before starting. Copy the "LEMON SHAKE-UP" game cards (Templates 9.6–9.9) onto the blank side of each of the four sheets, one template per sheet. Laminate the sheets and then cut the cards apart.

Gather together game board markers of the same eight colors used on the wheel and spokes. These may be plastic or paper (small squares or circles will do). Each table will need enough markers so that there is a marker for each player.

Decorate the program location using posters with positive self-esteem messages. These can usually be borrowed from teachers in the school as they are frequently used on many classroom bulletin boards. Or you may wish to re-create a particular setting from the novel such as the quarry, Tyler's bedroom, the principal's office, Buster's Game Room, or the park bench across from the police station. Whichever you choose, be sure to display a few lemons (either real, paper, or plastic) around the room or as table centerpieces.

Send copies of the invitation (Template 9.3) to each student who successfully completes your requirements for participation.

Assemble the facilitators' packets, one for each discussion table. Include a place card with the facilitator's name, a copy of the novel, the Agenda and Activity Instructions (Template 9.4), the Facilitator's Guide to Part 2 of the "LEMON SHAKE-UP" (Templates 9.10–9.12), and a thank-you note.

Confirm this list of materials for each table: a facilitator's packet, a game board, a deck of "LEMON SHAKE-UP" game cards, game board markers (one for each student), and a die.

Whetting Their Appetite

Select one of these program ideas to prepare your students for *The Trouble with Lemons* READ 'n' FEED program:

- Invite a mental health professional to talk to the students on the topic of self-esteem, introspection, or self-acceptance.

- Invite a school counselor to talk to the students about ways of "fitting in" at school, ways to establish new relationships, or ways to expand friendships and interests.

Mixing the Fiction, Food, and Fun

This program begins with the facilitator asking each person at the table to introduce himself or herself and to name a quality he or she considers important to friendship. Next, the facilitator should explain the rules for the game "LEMON SHAKE-UP" (Template 9.4). This game is designed to serve as a vehicle for discussing the novel without encouraging competition between the players. There is no winner of the game; all players answer questions about the novel and discuss the development of the main character. Students are each given a game board marker which they place on any space that matches its color. The first part of the discussion takes place as students take turns rolling a die and moving around the outer circle of the game board. Players move, draw a "LEMON SHAKE-UP" card, and read the question aloud. The students should be encouraged to give a complete answer; if the facilitator believes there can and should be more discussion, he or she should ask other players to comment on the question as well. Each player should take four or five turns or as long as the cards last. The second phase of the game, "LEMON SHAKE-UP" Part 2, begins when players begin to move along the spokes of the wheel toward the center. Players should position their markers at the outer end of the spoke that matches the color of their marker. Each player will roll the die and move that number of spaces along the spoke while citing examples from the novel that illustrate the concept printed on the spoke. The facilitator will have a list of some possible examples (Templates 9.10–9.12) and can evaluate others for correctness. The game is complete when all students have moved into the center hub of the game board, labeled SELF-ESTEEM.

Following "LEMON SHAKE-UP," one or two facilitators can booktalk the sequels to *The Trouble with Lemons*, which are *Eye of the Beholder* (Godine, 1992) and *No Effect* (Godine, 1994).

Hints for a Gourmet READ 'n' FEED

Set up a simple database report to make it easier for you to verify student participation and attendance, student homerooms, book circulation, and student testing results.

Plan on 45 to 60 minutes to complete this program: 10 minutes to serve food and begin eating; 5 minutes for table introductions and an explanation of the discussion format; 25 to 30 minutes to play "LEMON SHAKE-UP"; and 5 minutes for the booktalks.

Spray the room with lemon-scented air freshener just before the program begins.

Use the manual feed function on your copy machine to duplicate the templates for the game cards. You may wish to enlarge the templates before copying them to achieve cards closer to the size of regular playing cards. It is a good idea to laminate the cards and the game boards so that they can be used again.

Review the rules for "LEMON SHAKE-UP" with the students before beginning the discussion activity.

Don't forget to evaluate your program. Student and facilitator comments will help you revise future programs. A sample evaluation is included in the appendix of this book.

Novel Connections

Select one or more of these follow-up activities to extend the READ 'n' FEED program:

- Provide information to your students about counseling services available to teens both at school and in the community.
- Create a writing exercise for students: Ask them to brainstorm a new mystery featuring the main characters from the novel.

More Book Bites

Fleischman, Sid. *Rear-View Mirrors*. New York: Harper & Row, 1986.

Hayes, Daniel. *Eye of the Beholder*. Boston: Godine, 1992.

———. *No Effect*. Boston: Godine, 1994.

Kerr, M. E. *Night Kites*. New York: Harper & Row, 1986.

Peck, Richard. *Remembering the Good Times*. New York: Delacorte Press, 1985.

Voigt, Cynthia. *Izzy, Willy-Nilly*. New York: Atheneum, 1986.

Templates

Publicity Poster, Template 9.1

Flush Flash, Template 9.2

Student Invitation, Template 9.3

Agenda and Activity Instructions, Template 9.4

"LEMON SHAKE-UP" Game Card Backs, Template 9.5

"LEMON SHAKE-UP" Game Cards, Template 9.6

"LEMON SHAKE-UP" Game Cards, Template 9.7

"LEMON SHAKE-UP" Game Cards, Template 9.8

"LEMON SHAKE-UP" Game Cards, Template 9.9

Facilitator's Guide "LEMON SHAKE-UP" Part 2, Template 9.10

Facilitator's Guide "LEMON SHAKE-UP" Part 2, Template 9.11

Facilitator's Guide "LEMON SHAKE-UP" Part 2, Template 9.12

Booktalks for *Eye of the Beholder* and *No Effect*, Template 9.13

Hungry for a good book? Come to the . . .

Read 'n' Feed

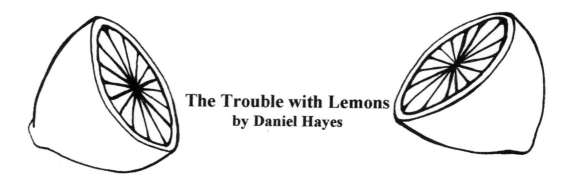

The Trouble with Lemons
by Daniel Hayes

Fiction:

The Trouble with Lemons

Food:

Fun:

Solve the mystery!

Date:

Time:

Place:

Sign up and pick up a copy of the book. For more details see

Template 9.1. Publicity Poster.

FLUSH FLASH

The Trouble with Lemons

by Daniel Hayes

Tyler is definitely not looking forward to being the new kid at school. But that becomes a minor problem after he finds the body . . . . the **dead body!**

He caught a brief glimpse of two people leaving the body . . . two murderers, who will need to make sure that Tyler doesn't talk. . . .

This book was written by an English teacher. His students gave him an
A+
An ALA Best Book

When you read, we feed!!!

Sponsored by

Date:

Do you mean lemons like lemons, the little yellow fruit??
No. Lemons like when something (or someone) is flawed, defective, messed up, impaired, imperfect, faulty, damaged, not working correctly, like call-in-the-repair-guys!

Find out what happens to Tyler and Lymie the night they decide to go skinny-dipping.

Sign up to read
The Trouble with Lemons
by Daniel Hayes.

Copies of the book are available

Be there! Don't be a lemon!

NO MORE BOO BOO?

Moe: Why did the cook stab the lemon with the knife?
Joe: I don't know, why?
Moe: It bitter.

Template 9.2. Flush Flash.

Due to the success of
last Saturday's
small party at the school pool

ANOTHER PARTY
will be held on

Date:_____

Time_____

Location:_____
Sign up limited
to those who have read
THE TROUBLE WITH LEMONS
Be there!

Due to the success of
last Saturday's
small party at the school pool

ANOTHER PARTY
will be held on

Date: _____

Time: _____

Location: _____
Sign up limited
to those who have read
THE TROUBLE WITH LEMONS
Be there!

Due to the success of
last Saturday's
small party at the school pool

ANOTHER PARTY
will be held on

Date: _____

Time: _____

Location:_____
Sign up limited
to those who have read
THE TROUBLE WITH LEMONS
Be there!

Due to the success of
last Saturday's
small party at the school pool

ANOTHER PARTY
will be held on

Date: _____

Time: _____

Location: _____
Sign up limited
to those who have read
THE TROUBLE WITH LEMONS
Be there!

Template 9.3. Student Invitation.

READ 'n' FEED
The Trouble with Lemons

AGENDA

_____	(10 min.)	Students receive seating assignments and meal; begin eating
_____	(2 min.)	Introductions; ask students to introduce themselves and to name qualities they consider important to friendship
_____	(3 min.)	Explanation of "LEMON SHAKE-UP"
_____	(25-30 min.)	Book discussion
_____	(5 min.)	Booktalks

Activity Instructions

Explain that the discussion of the novel will take place while playing "LEMON SHAKE-UP." Each table should have a game board, one die, and game markers for all the players. There is no winner of the game; all players answer questions about the novel and discuss the development of the main character, Tyler McAllister.

The discussion game is divided into two parts. **Part 1** focuses on answering questions about the novel. To begin, each participant should place his or her game board marker on any space on the outer circle of the board that matches the marker's color. The players take turns rolling a die and moving around the outer circle of the game board. The players move, draw a "LEMON SHAKE-UP" game card, and read the question aloud. The participants should be encouraged to give a complete answer. If you feel there can and should be more discussion, ask other players to comment on the question. Each player should take four or five turns or as long as the cards last.

Part 2 of the game begins when players begin to move down the spokes of the wheel toward the center of the game board. Players should position their markers at the outer end of the spoke that matches the color of their marker. Each player will roll the die and move that number of spaces along the spoke while citing examples from the novel that illustrate the concept printed on the spoke. A list of some possible examples is provided (Templates 9.10-9.12). Players may suggest other incidents from the novel that support the concepts.

The game is completed when all players have moved into the center hub of the game board, labeled "self-esteem."

Template 9.4. Agenda and Activity Instructions.

From *Fiction, Food, and Fun.* © 1998. Closter, Sipes, Thomas. Libraries Unlimited. (800) 237-6124.

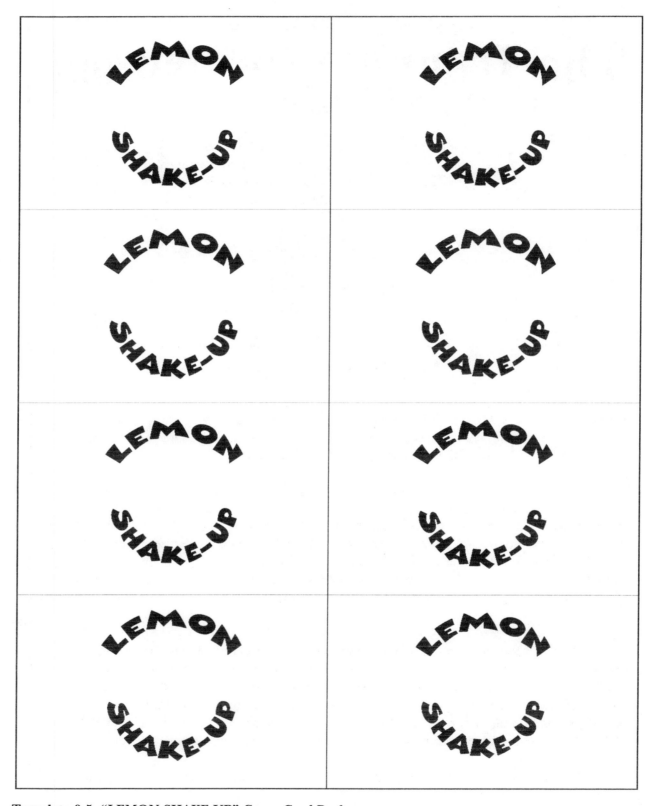

Template 9.5. "LEMON SHAKE-UP" Game Card Backs.

Why did Tyler think of himself as a lemon? 1	Describe the relationship between Tyler and Lymie. Why did they hang out together? 2
Lymie often disagrees with the actions Tyler takes. Does Tyler ever listen to Lymie? Would you? 3	Is it significant that Tyler dreams of his father after finding the body in the quarry? What do you think his dream means? 4
Discuss Tyler's reaction to the news of his father's death. 5	Tyler describes some students at his school as "loud, laughing kids who didn't have enough brains to be miserable. . . ." What does this tell you about Tyler? 6
Discuss what happened at Grant Academy. Relate what happened to Tyler's opinion of himself. 7	Tyler says he was not sticking up for Waller at Grant Academy when he got into so many fights. What was he fighting? 8

Template 9.6. "LEMON SHAKE-UP" Game Cards.

Why does Tyler regret that he "never got a chance to explain Grant Academy" to his father? What would he have told his father? 9	Discuss Tyler's decision to fight Beaver in gym class. Discuss his decision to face Beaver again after school. 10
What did Chuckie Deegan do that made Tyler feel that he wanted to adopt him into the family? 11	Why did Tyler want to hear about something stupid that Chuckie did? 12
Do you agree with Tyler when he says "maybe I was a born loser, some kind of unfixable lemon doomed to screw up, no matter what . . ."? Do you think he felt sorry for himself? 13	Tyler thinks his "whole life . . . (has) been so jinxed that hardly anything went right." Do you think this is a fair assessment? Do you think others are as organized and confident as they seem to Tyler? 14
Why do you think Tyler knocked Lymie down and begged to be forgiven for telling the "secret" to Mary Grace? 15	Tyler tells Mrs. Sanders, "I'm not trying to be perfect . . ." Do you think he is? 16

Template 9.7. "LEMON SHAKE-UP" Game Cards.

What do you think of the exchange between Mr. Blumberg and Mrs. Sanders? Who do you think made the best points? Were they both right?

17

How does Tyler feel after his outburst in Mr. Blumberg's office?

18

Do you think Chuckie is right when he tells Tyler that he is conceited?

19

What did Tyler tell Chuckie about the reason his father left the family?

20

What did Chuckie reveal to Tyler about the relationship between Tyler's parents? Why could Tyler believe what Chuckie said about Tyler's father's feelings when he hadn't listened to others telling him the same thing?

21

Do you think the Blumbergs were a believable family? Did the explanations for their behavior seem realistic?

22

Do you think the idea Tyler, Lymie, and Mary Grace came up with to pressure Jack to confess was a good one? Should they have called the police?

23

What helped Tyler the most in changing his low opinion of himself?

24

Template 9.8. "LEMON SHAKE-UP" Game Cards.

Do you think Chuckie's advice
to Tyler about not being a
"reactor" was good? Do you
think Tyler can change?

25

Why do you think Tyler felt he just
had to go to Buster's to find out if
Jack had confessed? Do you think
he put himself in danger?

26

Why did Jack choose to talk
to Tyler about what happened?

27

What motivated Tyler to sit across
from the police station while
Jack was inside?

28

Who do you think called Tyler's
mother to come home? Were
you surprised she showed up?

29

What did Tyler come to realize
about "good guys and bad guys"?

30

Do you think Tyler still views
himself as a lemon at the end of
story?

31

What did you like best about
this story? Would you
recommend it to a friend?

32

Template 9.9. "LEMON SHAKE-UP" Game Cards.

READ 'n' FEED
The Trouble with Lemons
Facilitator's Guide

LEMON SHAKE-UP, PART 2
Discussion Questions

The examples from the novel listed below are story incidents that relate to Tyler's development of positive self-esteem. These examples represent possible situations from the novel that players may offer to support one of the eight concepts of self-esteem as they move along the spokes of the game board. Players may offer examples from the novel not listed here and still be correct.

DEVELOP YOUR OWN VALUES	Tyler did not agree with Lymie that girls can't keep a secret—he talked to Mary Grace about his problems.
	Tyler did not avoid the after-school fight as others advised him because he believed he should get it over with.
	Tyler could not go along with the other students at the prep school who picked on Ralph Waller.
DON'T BE AFRAID TO TAKE RISKS	Tyler faced Beaver after school when he knew he was waiting for him.
	Tyler went to Mary Grace's house alone after dark when he suspected that Jack and Mark might be waiting outside his house.
	Tyler posted the announcement about the pool party to force Jack and Mark into action.
	Tyler went to Buster's to find out if Jack had been pushed to confess.
TURN SETBACKS INTO VICTORIES	After being "rescued" by Chuckie after the fight, Tyler discovered that Chuckie was a true friend.
	Tyler learned from Chuckie more about his family's true feelings after the confrontation in Mr. Blumberg's office.
	Tyler tried to call his brother after Mark and Jack attempt to drag him into their car—ended up talking to Mary Grace instead.

Template 9.10. Facilitator's Guide "LEMON SHAKE-UP" Part 2.

READ 'n' FEED
The Trouble with Lemons
Facilitator's Guide

LEMON SHAKE-UP, PART 2
Discussion Questions

The examples from the novel listed below are story incidents that relate to Tyler's development of positive self-esteem. These examples represent possible situations from the novel that players may offer to support one of the eight concepts of self-esteem as they move along the spokes of the game board. Players may offer examples from the novel not listed here and still be correct.

DEMAND RESPECT FROM OTHERS	Tyler stood up to Beaver and accused him of "slamming" during the touch football game.
	Tyler would not let Lymie put him down for sharing his problems with Mary Grace.
	Tyler gained Jack's respect by encouraging him to do the right thing.
	Tyler gained Mary Grace's respect for his openness.
SEEK FULFILLING RELATIONSHIPS	Tyler established open and honest dialogue with Chuckie regarding his feelings about his father, himself, and his experiences at school.
	Tyler accepted help and advice from Mary Grace.
	Tyler established a friendship with Lymie despite their differences.
ACCEPT WHO YOU ARE	Conversations with Chuckie helped Tyler accept himself (joke about wet pants and insight that he was not to blame for others' problems).
	Tyler had to deal with allergies.
	Tyler had to deal with having a famous mother and brother.
	Tyler had to deal with being teased about being a vegetarian.

Template 9.11. Facilitator's Guide "LEMON SHAKE-UP" Part 2.

READ 'n' FEED
The Trouble with Lemons
Facilitator's Guide
LEMON SHAKE-UP, PART 2
Discussion Questions

The examples from the novel listed below are story incidents that relate to Tyler's development of positive self-esteem. These examples represent possible situations from the novel that players may offer to support one of the eight concepts of self-esteem as they move along the spokes of the game board. Players may offer examples from the novel not listed here and still be correct.

AVOID BEING JUDGMENTAL	Tyler learned that Mr. Blumberg and Mark had problems and adjusted his thinking.
	Tyler understood that Lymie had his own reasons for not wanting to tell anyone that they found the body or saw a car pull away.
	Tyler made the effort to get along with Beaver after the fight.
	Tyler listened to and sympathized with Jack's position.
GIVE YOURSELF CREDIT	Tyler did not go along with the others at Grant Academy who harassed Ralph Waller.
	Tyler was unwilling to hide from the facts that suggested Mark and Jack were involved in BooBoo Anderson's death.
	Tyler was willing to learn from Chuckie about his weakness toward being a "reactor."
	Tyler showed courage when he stood up to Beaver's bullying.

Template 9.12. Facilitator's Guide "LEMON SHAKE-UP" Part 2.

Booktalk

Hayes, Daniel. *Eye of the Beholder*. Boston: Godine, 1992.

Tyler and Lymie are back. And in deep trouble. Maybe Tyler is right about how things just seem to happen to him. But to be fair, the whole thing was really Lymie's idea this time. Now Lymie doesn't get a lot of ideas, so it's easy to understand how he got so enthusiastic about his "big idea." His big idea was to become an artist and sell his art for megabucks. Tyler thought that sounded pretty good, too. They had seen some works by a famous sculptor who had once lived in their town, and they figured they could do as well as he did. But when their efforts didn't turn out too great, they chucked them into the river. That would have been the end of Lymie's artistic yearnings, except for the fact that the pieces were discovered and attributed to . . . none other than that famous sculptor Badoglio. Tyler and Lymie figured that it must have been because their works were so ugly that they looked like real art. Should they confess, or just keep their mouths shut and see what happens? After all, beauty is in the *Eye of the Beholder*.

Booktalk

Hayes, Daniel. *No Effect*. Boston: Godine, 1994.

There were many reasons why Tyler should not have gone out for wrestling. But the goofy-looking headgear and the crazy coach did not slow him down one bit. Those were just negatives to be overcome. After all, it would be worth it; he imagined himself in the middle of a crowd of adoring girls standing over his injured body with tears glistening in their eyes. Ah, the glory! He was a little bit uncomfortable with the possibility of getting seriously injured, though. That's why he talks his buddy, Lymie, into going along with him. And that's okay with Lymie. Sort of. Anyway, Tyler can't worry too much about wrestling; he has more important things to think about. Like his science teacher, with whom he has fallen hopelessly, helplessly, madly in love. He even begins calculating how many years it will take before their age difference won't matter. But then he makes a jaw-dropping discovery about her that jolts him more than any takedown he experiences in wrestling. *No Effect*? Big effect!

Template 9.13. Booktalks for *Eye of the Beholder* and *No Effect*.

Chapter 10

The View from the Cherry Tree

Bibliographic Information

Willo Davis Roberts. *The View from the Cherry Tree*. New York: Aladdin, 1993. 181 pages. $3.95. 0-689-717849.

Interest Level

Grades 6 through 8

Themes

Courage, Truth, Investigation, Respect, Family Relationships, Justice

Plot Summary

Although Rob tries to tell his family about the strange event that he witnessed next door, they are too busy with his sister's wedding to care. Rob knows that his cranky neighbor's death was no accident, but no one believes him—except the murderer. Rob must gather all his courage to outwit and expose the murderer before he becomes the next victim.

Author Information

Willo Davis Roberts is a prolific writer who has written almost 100 books during her career. She writes for children, young adults, and adults across several genres with the core of her work being mystery books. *The View from the Cherry Tree* (originally published in 1975), her first book for young readers, was originally written as an adult suspense novel. Her editor persuaded her to rewrite the story for children, and Roberts has enjoyed writing for a young audience ever since. She particularly enjoys the fan mail she receives from young people; she says their letters are invariably more rewarding than those from adults because children will more often tell her what they love about her books, not just what she did wrong.

Roberts began writing at a young age. Because her family moved around quite a bit when she was growing up, she turned to reading and writing as a refuge from the difficulties of changing schools and moving away from friends throughout her childhood. She published her first book after she was married and working with her husband to support their four children. Many of the experiences in her life are included in her stories; she often takes an incident, exaggerates it, and imagines how a character would react. She got the idea for *The View from the Cherry Tree* while preparing for the wedding of one of her daughters. It actually took her only two weeks to write this book, which has been popular with young people for more than 20 years. Roberts's lasting popularity may be partially attributed to her skill at building suspense; readers are hooked into the story from the first paragraph, and the pace never slows down.

Booktalk

I feel sorry for you if you've ever had a neighbor like Mrs. Calloway. Who's Mrs. Calloway? Well, she was Rob Mallory's neighbor. But the word *neighbor* is really too pleasant a word to describe Mrs. Calloway. Most of the kids who knew her had no problem believing that she caught children and ate them just like the witch did in the "Hansel and Gretel" story. She was nasty! And mean! She never had a nice word to say to anyone, she spied on people, she called the police if someone cut across her lawn or played a stereo too loudly, and she flat out tried to kill both Rob and his cat by attacking them with her broom! All he was doing when he got in so much trouble with everyone was just trying to pay her back. Well, anyway, it all backfired on him, so he decided to retreat to his favorite spot, the cherry tree. And that is how he happened to see her murder. But when he tries to tell his family about what he witnessed, no one seems to have the time to listen. No one except the murderer. Rob's *View from the Cherry Tree* may cost him his life!

What's Cookin' at the READ 'n' FEED?

This entertaining mystery is a perfect whodunit for middle school students. The program is designed around the interrogation of suspects who possibly committed the crime. Each participant, assuming the role of one of the six main characters of the story, is subpoenaed to appear for questioning. Students are instructed to come prepared to defend their character against the charge of murder. Their alibis must be based on facts from the novel. Students then rate their fellow suspects as to how well they defend their innocence. Role-playing is an effective discussion vehicle for this novel in that it allows participants to explore the characters and their motivations thoroughly.

Preparations

Check "The Recipe for a Successful READ 'n' FEED Program" at the beginning of this book for a discussion of those materials, design, resources, and handouts needed for every READ 'n' FEED program. Be sure to copy the Planning Outline and Program Checklist form in the appendix of this book so you will have it ready for your first design team meeting. In addition, this program requires props to create the atmosphere of a police interrogation room, a guest to interrogate the suspects, and score cards for participants to evaluate the suspects.

SHOPPING LIST

- Two portable partitions
- Black bulletin board paper
- Polaroid camera
- Portable spotlight
- Red construction paper
- Thread or fishing line
- Tree prop (live plant, artificial, or large branch)
- Plastic name tag covers with pins or clips
- Pencils
- Costume props for investigators
- Table coverings, plates, napkins, cups, dinnerware as needed
- Stool
- Black ink pads
- White card stock
- Sheets of blank paper
- A hat or container for drawing names

ADDING THE GARNISHES

- Check with your local police department to see if they have a film or video that explains the civil rights of suspects.
- Display career information in your library about police detectives.
- Invite a local police officer to the program to interrogate the "suspects."

FOOD FOR THOUGHT

Your menu for this novel should include cherries, if possible; perhaps cherry pie, cherry cobbler, cherry ice cream, cherry candy, or cherry soda. Other foods mentioned in the novel include sliced ham, salami, tuna sandwiches, chocolate cake, cookies, bologna sandwiches with mustard and Swiss cheese, catsup, pancakes, liver, hamburgers, peanut butter and jelly sandwiches, fried chicken, potato salad, buttered rolls, cauliflower, and carrot sticks.

WHIPPING UP THE FUN

Publicize the event at least a month in advance. Copy the Publicity Poster (Template 10.1) and Flush Flash (Template 10.2). Add your own local program details before displaying these templates. Write a promotional announcement for your school's daily announcements, calendar of events, or newspaper using the "Booktalk" or "Plot Summary" sections of this chapter. Distribute the book to the students along with information about the date of the program and any participation requirements. (See the sample Student Time Line Memo in the appendix at the end of this book.)

For the preliminary program, cut white card stock into 3-x-4-inch pieces. One piece is needed for each participant. Fold each piece in half horizontally so it will stand up on a table. A thumbprint of each participant is printed by inking the participant's thumb on an ink pad and pressing it onto a card. Add the student's name and assigned alias. There are six possible aliases to assign: Rob, Max, Derek, Darcy, Mr. Mallory, or Mrs. Mallory. Assign these aliases as evenly as possible.

Create "mug shots" of the participants by giving them each a Suspect Card (Template 10.4) to hold up at shoulder level while posing for a photograph. Use a Polaroid camera to create instant pictures. Assemble the mug shots into a collage to be displayed at the READ 'n' FEED program.

Produce name tags (Template 10.5) for Officers Riley and Fritz to wear while "processing" the suspects at the preliminary program and later at the READ 'n' FEED. The template also includes name tags for all of the "public defender" facilitators and the guest interrogator. The paper name tags can be slipped into plastic name tag holders which pin or clip to clothing.

Create an "Interrogation Room" by positioning two portable partitions at right angles to each other. Cover or drape the partitions with black bulletin board paper. Attach a portable spotlight to the top of one of the partitions. Place a stool in the center of the space created by the partitions. The entire prop should be positioned centrally so that everyone in the room can observe the suspect as he or she sits on the stool.

Make enough copies of the Character Score Card (Templates 10.7–10.8) so that each participant has one card for each of the six suspects. Place these on the tables for the facilitators to distribute. One cell on Template 10.8 is used by the facilitators to record the total score from each table for all suspects. You will need one Total Score card for each table. To avoid producing more Total Score cards than you need, fold Template 10.8 in half width-wise before copying. Make enough copies of the top half to match the number of participants. Make enough copies of the bottom half to match the number of tables. Supply enough pencils so each participant can have one.

Decorate a tree of some sort with cherries made from red construction paper and attached with thread or fishing line. Small tabletop trees or binoculars can be used as centerpieces on each table.

Send copies of the invitation (Template 10.3) to each student who successfully completes your requirements for participation.

Assemble the facilitators' packets, one for each table. Include a place card with the facilitator's name, a copy of the novel, the Agenda and Activity Instructions (Template 10.6), and a thank-you note.

Confirm this list of materials needed for each table: facilitator's packet, place cards for each student, six Character Score Cards for each student, one Total Score Card for the facilitator, six blank sheets of paper to record alibis, and a pencil for each student.

Whetting Their Appetites

The preliminary program for this READ 'n' FEED will generate excitement for what is to follow. Each participant is sent a "subpoena" (Template 10.3) which assigns to him or her a character from the novel whose identity he or she must assume. The character's name becomes the student's alias. The subpoena instructs the student to report to a specific room at a specified date and time to be fingerprinted. Treat the students as suspects who will soon be interrogated regarding their possible connection to the murder of Mrs. Calloway. Two of the volunteer facilitators will act as the "authorities," Officers Riley and Fritz. The officers should ink each student's thumb on the ink pad and print it on a piece of white card stock. Add the student's name and alias to the card. The cards are used at the program as seating place cards on the tables.

The next step is to photograph each suspect as if for a mug shot. The students hold up identification cards with numbers and the school's name (Template 10.4) for the picture. Display the mug shots later at the READ 'n' FEED program. After everyone has been fingerprinted and photographed, spend a few minutes explaining to the students the discussion format for the program. Because students will be asked to role-play their assigned character's defense against the charge of murder, they should be thinking about their character's alibi and motives.

Mixing the Fiction, Food, and Fun

As students arrive for the program, give them table assignments based on their aliases—six students, each representing a different character, and one facilitator are seated at each table. If your last table has fewer than six students, the discussion activity will not be affected. The discussion begins with a short brainstorming session at each table during which the facilitator, who assumes the role of a public defender, talks to the students about the defense each will use during the upcoming interrogation. Encourage the students to help each other develop an alibi based on information supported by the novel. The facts of the alibis can be listed on paper by a volunteer recorder at each table.

Following the brainstorming, the selection of the suspects for interrogation begins. Two facilitators, who have not been assigned to a discussion table, assume the roles of Officer Riley and Officer Fritz from the novel. The officers coordinate the selection by choosing at least one student from each table for questioning. This is done by drawing the names of the suspects from a hat. For example, if the first suspect on the list is called from the first table, then the next suspect on the list is called from the next table, and so on until all tables are represented among the six suspects who will be interrogated. In turn, each suspect takes his of her place on the stool in the "Interrogation Room" and answers the questions as accurately as possible based on his or her knowledge of the novel.

The actual interrogation of the suspects is conducted by a guest detective or investigator from the local police department. He or she asks questions (Templates 10.9–10.14) and tries to determine whom to arrest for the crime. During the interrogation, the other students listen and evaluate the suspect's credibility and adherence to the information about the character and the crime supplied by the novel. They then complete Character Score Cards (Templates 10.7–10.8), which they pass to the table facilitators at the end of each interrogation. The facilitators tally the scores during the interrogations so that when all the questioning is finished, a composite score from each table for each suspect is ready for the interrogator. The interrogator, who has not read the novel, uses his or her impressions from the questioning as well as the ratings by the audience to decide whom to arrest for the murder of Mrs. Calloway. After the interrogator announces his or her conclusion, he or she and the students can talk informally about the case and how the decision was made.

As a wrap-up for the discussion of this novel, the guest police officer can briefly describe police procedures regarding questioning suspects and investigating crimes.

Hints for a Gourmet READ 'n' FEED

Set up a simple database report to make it easier for you to verify student participation and attendance, student homerooms, book circulation, and student testing results.

The role-play format for this program allows for creativity and flexibility in determining how much drama to introduce into the book discussion. Encourage the facilitators to set the tone through costumes and props. The table facilitators can dress as lawyers and pass out business cards. Officers Riley and Fritz can wear uniforms and badges. These characters can set the stage for the interrogation when they select the suspects for questioning. The mood can be comical or serious, depending on which works best for your audience. The officers escort each suspect to the "Interrogation Room."

The students enjoy the fingerprinting and mug shots at the preliminary program, and this is a great opportunity to build up excitement for this particular program and general interest throughout the student body. Be aware that the subpoena, which serves to invite the students to the preliminary program, can confuse those unfamiliar with the program. We were very surprised when a parent called to ask why his child was being questioned!

Be sure to let your guest police detective know what sort of tone to assume during the questioning. To best carry out the whodunit theme of this novel, the interrogator should not know beforehand who committed the crime.

Plan on at least 45 minutes to complete this program: 10 minutes to serve the meal and to seat the students, 10 minutes for brainstorming a defense, 20 minutes for the interrogations, and 5 minutes for a wrap-up.

Don't forget to evaluate your program. Student and facilitator comments will help you revise future programs. A sample evaluation form is included in the appendix at the end of this book.

Novel Connections

Select one or more of these follow-up activities to extend the READ 'n' FEED program:

- Ask a local law enforcement official to talk to the students about what they can do if they become aware that someone they know is involved with drugs.

- Invite a mental health professional to talk to the students about communication patterns within families or about how stress (that comes from a big event like a wedding) affects families.

- Build on the interest in Rob's attachment to his cat by offering students the opportunity to talk about their pets, write about their pets, or perhaps hold a "Pet Photo" contest.

More Book Bites

Avi. *Wolf Rider: A Tale of Terror.* New York: Bradbury Press, 1986.

Duncan, Lois. *I Know What You Did Last Summer.* Boston: Little Brown, 1973.

Kerr, M. E. *Fell Down.* New York: HarperCollins, 1991.

Nixon, Joan Lowery. *Spirit Seeker.* New York: Delacorte Press, 1995.

Wilde, Nicholas. *Death Knell.* New York: Henry Holt, 1991.

Windsor, Patricia. *The Christmas Killer.* New York: Scholastic, 1991.

Templates

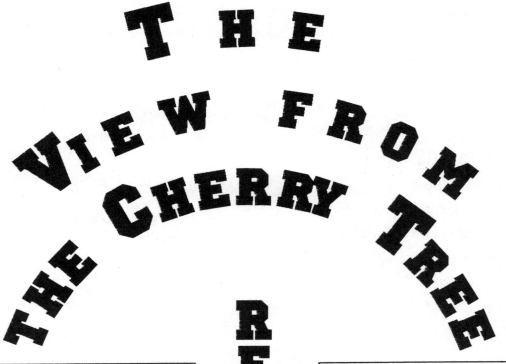

THE VIEW FROM THE CHERRY TREE

READ 'N' FEED

Fiction:
THE VIEW FROM
THE CHERRY TREE
by Willo Davis Roberts

Food:

Fun:
You better have a
good alibi or **you** may
be charged with THE
CRIME!

When:

Where:

How:
Sign up before it's
too late! Pick up a
copy of the book right
away!

Template 10.1. Publicity Poster.

FLUSH FLASH

The View from the Cherry Tree

by Willo Davis Roberts

Sitting in a cherry tree, trying to spit cherry pits into a neighbor's window, just seems like good, harmless fun. So why does it lead to Rob being shot at, almost poisoned, nearly pushed out a third-story window, and just about trapped in a burning building?

> How do you feel about **SPIDERS?**

Find out what happens to Rob when no one listens as he tries to tell them about the murder next door.

Sign up to read
THE VIEW FROM THE CHERRY TREE
by Willo Davis Roberts

Copies of the book are available.

Date:

So where does a 22 pound cat sit?
Anywhere it wants to!

Meet MRS. CALLOWAY, the meanest person on earth

"She's a witch . . . she eats raw liver!"
—Rob Mallory

"She's mean enough to poison herself on her own spit."
—Max

"It's the only thing I don't like about this house. Having her for a neighbor."
—Mrs. Mallory

When you read, we feed!!!

Sponsored by

Template 10.2. Flush Flash.

From *Fiction, Food, and Fun.* © 1998. Closter, Sipes, Thomas. Libraries Unlimited. (800) 237-6124.

SUBPOENA

_____   _____
(name)   (alias)

You are wanted for questioning in the murder of
Mrs. Calloway. In accordance with the laws of the
State of _____ you must:

First: Report to _____ of this building for
                                 (room)
             fingerprinting and instructions on

             _____ at _____.
                      (date)   (time)

Second: Report to _____ of this building on
                                  (room)

             _____ at _____ and
                      (date)   (time)
             be prepared to prove your innocence from

             _____ point of VIEW (FROM
                      (alias)
             THE CHERRY TREE).

Failure to appear at these times will result in your immediate
incarceration.

Signed,

Officer Riley
Officer Fritz

Template 10.3. Student Invitation.

From _Fiction, Food, and Fun._ © 1998. Closter, Sipes, Thomas. Libraries Unlimited. (800) 237-6124.

343768456

794420539

Template 10.4. Suspect Card.

CITY POLICE DEPARTMENT

Homicide Division

Officer Riley

Special Investigator

CITY POLICE DEPARTMENT

Homicide Division

Officer Fritz

Special Investigator

CITY POLICE DEPARTMENT

Homicide Division

Special Investigator

PROFESSIONAL LEGAL SERVICES

Criminal Defense

Attorney at Law

PROFESSIONAL LEGAL SERVICES

Criminal Defense

Attorney at Law

PROFESSIONAL LEGAL SERVICES

Criminal Defense

Attorney at Law

PROFESSIONAL LEGAL SERVICES

Criminal Defense

Attorney at Law

PROFESSIONAL LEGAL SERVICES

Criminal Defense

Attorney at Law

Template 10.5. Facilitator's Name Tags.

READ 'n' FEED
The View from the Cherry Tree

AGENDA

_____ (10 min.) Students receive seating assignments and meal; begin eating.
_____ (10 min.) Brainstorming.
_____ (2 min.) Selection of characters for interrogation.
_____ (20 min.) Interrogation.
_____ (2 min.) Conclusion and arrest.
_____ (5 min.) Wrap-up.

Activity Instructions

During the brainstorming session, facilitators who have been assigned to a table will assume the role of a public defender. Each of the six students at the table will play the role of a character from the novel. All have been informed that they are suspects in the murder of Mrs. Calloway. The facilitators will talk to the suspects about their defense and their alibis in preparation for the upcoming interrogation. Ask one of the students at the table to serve as a recorder. The recorder will write down key points of each character's defense. Encourage all the characters to help each other prepare their defense based on the facts and information provided in the novel.

Two facilitators who have not been assigned to a table will assume the roles of Officers Riley and Fritz from the novel. The officers will select a character from each table to be interrogated. A different character will be selected from each table until all six suspects are represented. The suspect may take his or her alibi notes to the interrogation.

The interrogator will ask each suspect questions. During the interrogation, the other students will evaluate how well the suspect defends himself or herself. Each student will complete a Character Score Card for each suspect. The number listed after each rating will be used to calculate the character's score. The score cards should then be passed to the table facilitator. As the next interrogation begins, the facilitator will tally the scores and record the total score for the suspect on a score card, which will be given to the interrogator after all six suspects have been questioned. The interrogator will use the totals from each table, plus his or her own impressions, to decide whom to arrest for the murder of Mrs. Calloway.

Template 10.6. Agenda and Activity Instructions.

CHARACTER SCORE CARD

Darcy

Rate your fellow suspects as to how well they defend their innocence.

Was the character believable?

____Yes (2) ____Sometimes (1) ____No (0)

Did the character answer the questions according to the book?

____Yes (2) ____Sometimes (1) ____No (0)

Did the character appear to be withholding or hiding information?

____No (2) ____Sometimes (1) ____Yes (0)

Total score _____

CHARACTER SCORE CARD

Rob

Rate your fellow suspects as to how well they defend their innocence.

Was the character believable?

____Yes (2) ____Sometimes (1) ____No (0)

Did the character answer the questions according to the book?

____Yes (2) ____Sometimes (1) ____No (0)

Did the character appear to be withholding or hiding information?

____No (2) ____Sometimes (1) ____Yes (0)

Total score _____

CHARACTER SCORE CARD

Derek

Rate your fellow suspects as to how well they defend their innocence.

Was the character believable?

____Yes (2) ____Sometimes (1) ____No (0)

Did the character answer the questions according to the book?

____Yes (2) ____Sometimes (1) ____No (0)

Did the character appear to be withholding or hiding information?

____No (2) ____Sometimes (1) ____Yes (0)

Total score _____

CHARACTER SCORE CARD

Max

Rate your fellow suspects as to how well they defend their innocence.

Was the character believable?

____Yes (2) ____Sometimes (1) ____No (0)

Did the character answer the questions according to the book?

____Yes (2) ____Sometimes (1) ____No (0)

Did the character appear to be withholding or hiding information?

____No (2) ____Sometimes (1) ____Yes (0)

Total score _____

Template 10.7. Character Score Card.

CHARACTER SCORE CARD

Mrs. Mallory

Rate your fellow suspects as to how well they defend their innocence.

Was the character believable?

____Yes (2) ____Sometimes (1) ____No (0)

Did the character answer the questions according to the book?

____Yes (2) ____Sometimes (1) ____No (0)

Did the character appear to be withholding or hiding information?

____No (2) ____Sometimes (1) ____Yes (0)

Total score _____

CHARACTER SCORE CARD

Mr. Mallory

Rate your fellow suspects as to how well they defend their innocence.

Was the character believable?

____Yes (2) ____Sometimes (1) ____No (0)

Did the character answer the questions according to the book?

____Yes (2) ____Sometimes (1) ____No (0)

Did the character appear to be withholding or hiding information?

____No (2) ____Sometimes (1) ____Yes (0)

Total score _____

CHARACTER SCORE CARD

TOTALS

_____ **Rob**

_____ **Derek**

_____ **Max**

_____ **Darcy**

_____ **Mrs. Mallory**

_____ **Mr. Mallory**

Table # _____

CHARACTER SCORE CARD

TOTALS

_____ **Rob**

_____ **Derek**

_____ **Max**

_____ **Darcy**

_____ **Mrs. Mallory**

_____ **Mr. Mallory**

Table # _____

Template 10.8. Character Score Card.

READ 'n' FEED
The View from the Cherry Tree
Facilitator's Guide

Interrogation Questions

Rob

How would you describe your relationship with Mrs. Calloway?

Tell us what happened when you followed your cat over to Mrs. Calloway's back porch the day before she was killed. Isn't it true that you told others that she had deliberately put meat scraps in the garbage to lure your cat onto her property? Why did she attack you with a broom if it was the cat she was after?

Why didn't your parents call the police after she attacked you? Did this upset you? Did you swear to seek revenge?

We have a witness who says you hoped you could scare Mrs. Calloway into having a fit by finding you "dead" at the foot of her back steps. Why did you want her to think you were dead? Did you get into trouble for this trick? Did it make you even more angry with Mrs. Calloway? So angry you wanted to kill her?

Where were you at the time of the murder? What were you doing? We have a witness who overheard a conversation in which she referred to "that nasty little boy." Was she referring to you? Isn't it possible that you were so angry that you threw a cherry at her, which caused her to lean out the window to see who did it and fall?

During the investigation we found numerous spiders in the tower room of Mrs. Calloway's house. Don't you have a spider collection? Isn't it possible that you released your spiders in her house several hours before she fell out the window and that one of them bit her, causing her to fall?

Template 10.9. Interrogation Questions for Rob.

From *Fiction, Food, and Fun.* © 1998. Closter, Sipes, Thomas. Libraries Unlimited. (800) 237-6124.

READ 'n' FEED
The View from the Cherry Tree
Facilitator's Guide

Interrogation Questions

Max

How many years did you know Mrs. Calloway?

Are you aware that Mrs. Calloway called the police station to complain about your habit of parking in front of her house? Why did you always park there?

Were you trying to intimidate her on the day you ran over her garden hose? Did she make you so angry with her threats to call the police about the hose that you lost control of yourself?

Isn't it true that you said Mrs. Calloway was "mean enough to poison herself on her own spit?" What did you mean by that? Did you ever think of poisoning her? Do you know anything about the piece of poisoned chicken that was found?

Witnesses say that you parked your car around the corner from Mrs. Calloway's house the day of the murder. Why did you park around the corner on that particular day?

Where were you at the time of the murder? How did you manage to arrive at the scene so quickly after her body was discovered?

We have witnesses who will testify that you said you "weren't sorry that the old biddy has cashed in" and that you were "tempted to push her" out the window yourself. Did you kill Mrs. Calloway?

Template 10.10. Interrogation Questions for Max.

From *Fiction, Food, and Fun.* © 1998. Closter, Sipes, Thomas. Libraries Unlimited. (800) 237-6124.

READ 'n' FEED
The View from the Cherry Tree
Facilitator's Guide

Interrogation Questions

Derek

What was your relationship with your aunt? Did you visit her often?

Why were you at the Mallorys' house the day of the murder? Did you hold your aunt responsible for Darcy breaking off your engagement? Are you still in love with Darcy?

Did your aunt have any enemies in the neighborhood?

Where were you at the time of the murder? Were you with anyone who can verify your alibi?

What did you feel when you heard the news of Mrs. Calloway's death? Why didn't you go home to be with your mother after you heard the news?

How did you get those scratches on your arm?

Rob says you were looking for something in Mrs. Calloway's house. What were you looking for?

Did you try to burn down Mrs. Calloway's house?

Why were you in the tower room with Rob? Is it true you threatened his life? Why is he so frightened of you?

Template 10.11. Interrogation Questions for Derek.

From *Fiction, Food, and Fun.* © 1998. Closter, Sipes, Thomas. Libraries Unlimited. (800) 237-6124.

READ 'n' FEED
The View from the Cherry Tree
Facilitator's Guide

> **Interrogation Questions**
>
> ### Darcy

How did you feel about Mrs. Calloway as a neighbor? Did you ever have a confrontation with her?

How did you feel about the way Mrs. Calloway treated your brother?

Is it true that you thought your mom and dad should have called the police when Mrs. Calloway attacked Rob? Did it make you angry that no one was doing anything about it?

Weren't you pretty upset that Rob was going to have a black eye in your wedding pictures? Did you go over to Mrs. Calloway's house to talk to her about what she had done to spoil your wedding?

Isn't it true that you were sneaking over to Mrs. Calloway's house to cause some mischief when you saw Rob lying at the foot of her back steps? Didn't you start screaming so that no one would suspect what you were really doing?

Some people say that you wanted to be sure that Mrs. Calloway didn't cause a scene during your wedding, so you went next door to talk to her just before her body was discovered. Is that true?

Is it true that when you were engaged to Derek you developed a hatred for Mrs. Calloway because she said you weren't good enough to marry anyone in her family?

Template 10.12. Interrogation Questions for Darcy.

From *Fiction, Food, and Fun.* © 1998. Closter, Sipes, Thomas. Libraries Unlimited. (800) 237-6124.

READ 'n' FEED
The View from the Cherry Tree
Facilitator's Guide

Interrogation Questions
Mr. Mallory

Why didn't you want to call the police after Mrs. Calloway injured your son? Did you think you were going to take care of it yourself?

Were you seriously going to let the fact that your family was preparing for a wedding take precedence over your son's safety? Mrs. Calloway deliberately attacked an 11-year-old boy! Didn't you want to see her punished?

If you thought Mrs. Calloway was "certifiably" crazy, how could you put your family at risk by doing nothing? Didn't you decide to do something to keep her from hurting anyone else?

Witnesses say you were really angry with Rob when he tried to make Mrs. Calloway think he was dead. Were you angry because he messed up your plans to get even with her?

Is it true that you hoped to buy Mrs. Calloway's house for your daughter Darcy and her husband?

Some people have said that Mrs. Calloway might have been blackmailing you about something that happened a long time ago and that is why you put up with her abuse of your family. Is that true?

Where were you at the time of the murder? Can you prove it?

Template 10.13. Interrogation Questions for Mr. Mallory.

READ 'n' FEED
The View from the Cherry Tree
Facilitator's Guide

Interrogation Questions

Mrs. Mallory

Is it true that you said. "It's the only thing I don't like about this house. Having her for a neighbor"? Why didn't you like Mrs. Calloway?

Is it true that you and Mrs. Calloway exchanged many angry words about the mess the cherries from the cherry tree made in her yard?

Witnesses say that you called Mrs. Calloway "an old witch" and wanted your husband to call the police after she attacked Rob. Did you decide to take care of the matter yourself?

Weren't you afraid that your husband wasn't going to do anything about Mrs. Calloway and you couldn't stand the idea of her "getting away" with injuring your son?

Isn't it true that you got sick of Mrs. Calloway always peering into your house with her binoculars and that you threatened to strangle her with them?

People say that you wanted Darcy's wedding to be perfect. Were you worried that Mrs. Calloway would do something to ruin all your plans and hard work?

Where were you at the time of the murder? Can anyone verify that?

Template 10.14. Interrogation Questions for Mrs. Mallory.

From *Fiction, Food, and Fun.* © 1998. Closter, Sipes, Thomas. Libraries Unlimited. (800) 237-6124.

Appendix:

READ 'n' FEED Forms

The examples in this appendix will help you plan, organize, and evaluate your READ 'n' FEED program. The Planning Outline and Program Checklist serves as a working agenda for design team meetings, includes space for you to record brainstorming ideas, makes it easy note team responsibilities, and provides a box to check off completed tasks. The sample Student Time Line Memo gives stduents a schedule of program expectations by which they can budget their reading time. The READ 'n' FEED Program Evaluation is one way to get feedback from your participants about the effectiveness of your programming efforts. Because each community of readers has different needs, interests, and available resources, their comments need to influence your planning of Future READ 'n' FEED programs.

READ 'n' FEED Planning Outline and Program Checklist

Title with bibliographic information: _____

_____

☐ Quantity ordered: _____

☐ Cost: _____

☐ Date: _____

1. Timeline (dates)

☐ Team planning meeting #1: _____

☐ Team planning meeting #2: _____

☐ Team planning meeting #3: _____

☐ Sign-up and book distribution: _____

☐ Quiz deadline: _____

☐ Preliminary program: _____

☐ READ 'n' FEED: _____

Continued on next page.

From *Fiction, Food, and Fun.* © 1998. Closter, Sipes, Thomas. Libraries Unlimited. (800) 237-6124.

2. Publicity

☐ Announcement/booktalk for sign-up day _____

_____

☐ Publicity posters _____

_____

☐ Flush Flash _____

_____

☐ Timeline reminder announcements _____

_____

3. Book Distribution

☐ Books stamped and processed for checkout _____

_____

☐ Student sign-up sheet _____

_____

☐ Student timeline memo _____

_____

4. Description of program

☐ Theme: _____

_____

☐ Outline of program: _____

_____

☐ Discussion strategies (what students will do/what facilitators will do): _____

_____

☐ Discussion questions: _____

_____

☐ Preliminary program: _____

_____

☐ Location: _____

_____

☐ Room arrangement: _____

_____

☐ Decorations: _____

_____

5. Supplies: _____

_____

_____

_____

6. Resources

☐ Discussion facilitators: _____

_____

_____

☐ Copy of novel with discussion questions and any special instructions: _____

_____

☐ Community speakers or guests: _____

_____

☐ Related books: _____

_____

☐ Media: _____

_____

Continued on next page.

☐ Equipment: _____

_____

7. Food

☐ Restaurant or sponsor: _____

☐ Contact person: _____

☐ Menu: _____

_____

☐ Location: _____

☐ Delivery or carryout arrangements: _____

_____

☐ Drinks: _____

8. Program preparation and assembly

☐ Activity templates, game boards, cards, etc. _____

_____

☐ Student accountability (e.g., book quiz, parent permission) _____

_____

☐ Student invitations _____

_____

☐ Guest invitations _____

_____

☐ Agenda and activity instructions _____

_____

☐ Facilitator packets _____

_____

☐ Documentation of program (e.g., 35mm, video, still video, local news media coverage)

_____

_____

☐ Thank-you notes for facilitators _____

_____

☐ Thank-you banner for sponsor(s) _____

_____

☐ Program evaluation by participants _____

_____

9. **Additional arrangements or assignments:** _____

_____

_____

10. **Novel connections (optional planning):** _____

_____

_____

Sample Student Time Line Memo

READ 'n' FEED
March 26, _____
Don't Look Behind You by Lois Duncan

Dear Student,

Please read this program time line carefully. You will need to know these deadlines to successfully complete the requirements for participation in the March 26th READ 'n' FEED program.

March 1–March 5: Sign up in the media center.

March 1–March 19: Read *Don't Look Behind You.*

March 17–19: Take book quiz in the media center during homeroom one of these days.

March 19, end of B Lunch: Make sure your quiz is taken.

March 24, homeroom: Look for your invitation if you complete and pass the requirements.

March 25: Attend READ 'n' FEED preliminary program in the auditorium during homeroom.

March 26, Lunch: Enjoy the READ 'n' FEED!!!!!

If you have any questions concerning this memo, please contact _____.

READ 'n' FEED Program Evaluation

Title:

Date:

Under each statement, circle the feeling that most agrees with your attitude toward the program.

1. **I enjoyed reading this novel.**

   Strongly agree   Agree somewhat   Disagree

2. **I thought my table had an interesting discussion of the novel.**

   Strongly agree   Agree somewhat   Disagree

3. **I was able to participate in the discussion.**

   Strongly agree   Agree somewhat   Disagree

4. **I enjoyed the program activity.**

   Strongly agree   Agree somewhat   Disagree

5. **I was motivated to read knowing that food was donated by**

   _____

   Strongly agree   Agree somewhat   Disagree

6. **I will recommend this novel to a friend.**

   Strongly agree   Agree somewhat   Disagree

7. **I will recommend participating in a READ 'n' FEED to a friend.**

   Strongly agree   Agree somewhat   Disagree

Continued on next page.

Please complete the following statements.

8. **My favorite part of the READ 'n' FEED was** _____

_____

9. **I wish we would have had more time to** _____

10. **I suggest these changes for future READ 'n' FEED programs:** _____

_____

11. **I recommend this restaurant or food as a future sponsor:** _____

_____

12. **I would like to recommend this title for a future program:** _____

_____

Name (optional): _____

Bibliography of Young Adult Literature Resources

Blostein, Fay. *Invitations, Celebrations: Ideas and Techniques for Promoting Reading in Junior and Senior High Schools.* New York: Neal-Schuman, 1993.

Bodart, Joni Richards. *Booktalk! 2: Booktalking for All Ages and Audiences.* New York: H. W. Wilson, 1985.

———. *Booktalk! 3: More Booktalks for All Ages and Audiences.* New York: H. W. Wilson, 1988.

———. *Booktalk! 4: Selections from* The Booktalker *for All Ages and Audiences.* New York: H. W. Wilson, 1992.

———. *Booktalk! 5: More Selections from* The Booktalker *for All Ages and Audiences.* New York: H. W. Wilson, 1993.

———. *100 World-Class Thin Books, or, What to Read When Your Book Report Is Due Tomorrow!* Englewood, CO: Libraries Unlimited, 1993.

De Vos, Gail. *Storytelling for Young Adults: Techniques and Treasury.* Englewood, CO: Libraries Unlimited, 1991.

Drew, Bernard A. *The 100 Most Popular Young Adult Authors: Biographical Sketches and Bibliographies.* 1st rev. ed. Englewood, CO: Libraries Unlimited, 1997.

Estes, Sally. *Genre Favorites for Young Adults: A Collection of* Booklist *Columns.* Chicago: American Library Association, 1993.

Gallo, Donald R., ed. *Literature for Teenagers: New Books, New Approaches.* Bozrah, CT: Connecticut Council for Teachers of English, 1993.

———. *Speaking for Ourselves: Autobiographical Sketches by Notable Authors of Books for Young Adults.* Urbana, IL: National Council of Teachers of English, 1990.

———. *Speaking for Ourselves Too: More Autobiographical Sketches by Notable Authors of Books for Young Adults.* Urbana, IL: National Council of Teachers of English, 1993.

Gillespie, John Thomas, ed. *Best Books for Senior High Readers.* New Providence, NJ: R. R. Bowker, 1991.

Gillespie, John Thomas, and Corinne Naden. *Juniorplots 4: A Booktalk Guide for Use with Readers, Ages 12–16.* New Providence, NJ: R. R. Bowker, 1993.

———. *The Newbery Companion: Booktalk and Related Materials for Newbery Materials for Newbery Medal and Honor Books.* Englewood, CO: Libraries Unlimited, 1996.

Hall, Susan. *Using Picture Storybooks to Teach Literary Devices: Recommended Books for Children and Young Adults.* Phoenix, AZ: Oryx Press, 1994.

Herald, Diana Tixier. *Teen Genreflecting.* Englewood, CO: Libraries Unlimited, 1997.

Herz, Sarah K. *From Hinton to Hamlet: Building Bridges Between Young Adult Literature and the Classics.* Westport, CT: Greenwood, 1996.

Immell, Myra, ed. *The Young Adult Reader's Adviser.* 2 vols. New Providence, NJ: R. R. Bowker, 1992.

Johnson, Lauri, and Sally Smith. *Dealing with Diversity Through Multicultural Fiction.* Chicago: American Library Association, 1993.

Jones, Patrick. *Connecting Young Adults and Libraries: A How-to-Do-It Manual.* New York: Neal-Schuman, 1992.

Kaywell, Joan F. *Adolescents at Risk: A Guide to Fiction and Nonfiction for Young Adults, Parents, and Professionals.* Westport, CT: Greenwood, 1993.

Kennedy, DayAnn M., Stella S. Spangler, and Mary Ann Vanderwerf. *Science and Technology in Fact and Fiction: A Guide to Young Adult Books.* New York: R. R. Bowker, 1990.

Kies, Cosette. *Supernatural Fiction: More Than 1300 Good Paperbacks to Read for Wonderment, Fear, and Fun.* 2d ed. Englewood, CO: Libraries Unlimited, 1992.

Krashen, Stephen D. *The Power of Reading: Insights from the Research.* Englewood, CO: Libraries Unlimited, 1992.

Kutenplon, Deborah, and Ellen Olmstead. *Young Adult Fiction by African American Writers, 1968–1993: A Critical and Annotated Guide.* New York: Garland, 1996.

Latrobe, Kathy H., and Mildred Laughlin. *Readers Theatre for Young Adults: Scripts and Script Development.* Englewood, CO: Teacher Ideas Press, 1989.

Lynn, Ruth Nadelman. *Fantasy Literature for Children and Young Adults: An Annotated Bibliography.* New York: R. R. Bowker, 1995.

Pellowski, Anne. *The Storytelling Handbook: A Young People's Collection of Unusual Tales and Helpful Hints on How to Tell Them.* New York: Simon & Schuster Books for Young Readers, 1995.

Phelan, Patricia, ed. *High Interest Easy Reading: An Annotated Booklist for Middle and Senior High School.* Urbana, IL: National Council of Teachers of English, 1996.

Polette, Nancy. *Novel Booktalks: Award Winners and Other Favorites.* O'Fallon, MO: Book Lures, 1992.

Reed, Arthea J. *Comics to Classics: A Parent's Guide to Books for Teens and Preteens.* Newark, DE: International Reading Association, 1988.

Rochman, Hazel. *Against Borders: Promoting Books for a Multicultural World.* Chicago: American Library Association, 1993.

———. *Tales of Love and Terror: Booktalking the Classics, Old and New.* Chicago: American Library Association, 1987.

Rosow, La Vergne. *Light 'n Lively Reads for ESL, Adult, and Teen Readers: A Thematic Bibliography.* Englewood, CO: Libraries Unlimited, 1996.

Samuels, Barbara, and G. Kylene Beers, eds. *Your Reading: An Annotated Booklist for Middle School and Junior High.* Urbana, IL: National Council of Teachers of English, 1996.

Sherman, Gale W., and Bette D. Ammon. *Rip-Roaring Reads for Reluctant Teen Readers.* Englewood, CO: Libraries Unlimited, 1993.

Spencer, Pam. *What Do Young Adults Read Next? A Reader's Guide to Fiction for Young Adults.* Detroit: Gale Research, 1994.

Trelease, Jim. *Read All About It! Great Read-Aloud Stories, Poems, and Newspaper Pieces for Preteens and Teens.* New York: Penguin Books, 1993.

Walker, Elinor. *Book Bait: Detailed Notes on Adult Books Popular with Young People.* Chicago: American Library Association, 1988.

Zvirin, Stephanie. *The Best Years of Their Lives: A Resource Guide for Teenagers in Crisis.* Chicago: American Library Association, 1992.